CA...

HOW to Write a GREAT Story

First published in Great Britain in 2019 by
PICCADILLY PRESS
80–81 Wimpole St, London W1G 9RE
www.piccadillypress.co.uk

A CIP catalogue record for this book is available
from the British Library.

ISBN: 978-1-84812-814-9
Also available as an ebook

1

Designed by Sue Michniewicz
Printed and bound in Great Britain by Clays Ltd, Elcograf S.p.A.

Piccadilly Press is an imprint of Bonnier Books UK
www.bonnierbooks.co.uk

TO MY MENTOR,
JOHN TRUBY

'When I read a good book I wish that life were three thousand years long.'
Ralph Waldo Emerson

FOREWORD

In this book I share all my secrets and practical advice for writing a great story. And by 'story', I don't just mean a book. Your story could be a movie. It could also be a platform game, a music video, a play, a graphic novel, a ballet or even a tale told out loud to your friends or family. Almost all my tips come from screenwriters or filmmakers because they are the ones who have helped me the most.

In part one, I start with an introduction that tells how I started writing, came up with ideas and got published.

I include my revelations about **Writing on the Right Side of the Brain**.

I briefly give examples of three **Sample Workshops**.

I finish with a short account of **My Daily Writer's Routine** and thoughts about **How Your Story Could Change the World**.

In part two, I've also tossed in over a hundred quick tips, tricks and tropes that writers know about and that you might enjoy using. A 'trope' is a storytelling device. **Magpie**, **Cup of Cocoa** and **Rubber Ducky**

are just three examples. These are in **bold letters** to show that you can look them up in part two, where they are listed alphabetically and I talk about them in more detail.

This book is aimed at storytellers of any age, from children to adults, including teachers. Think of this book as a treasure chest full of gems. Or, better yet, a refrigerator full of all sorts of food. You can just pop by for an inspirational snack or make a whole meal from its ingredients.

If you find this book useful, I ask only one thing: that you invite me to your book launch or movie premier.

Happy writing!

Caroline Lawrence

"Literature is a LUXURY,

Fiction is a Necessity."

G.K. Chesterton

THE BEST JOB IN THE WORLD

Being a writer is the best job in the world.

You can sit around all morning in your pyjamas, drinking hot chocolate and making up stories . . . and people pay you to do it!

In the afternoons you can go to the movies and call it 'research'. In the evenings you can watch TV and call it 'research'. And of course you can read as many books as you like.

So how do you become a writer?

Writing is a skill, and like every skill it requires practice, dedication and self-discipline.

A few people are born storytellers, but the rest of us have to learn.

WHO WHERE WHAT

There are three main aspects of any story: the **WHO**, the **WHAT** and the **WHERE**. The characters are **WHO** the story is about. The setting is **WHERE** it takes place. And the plot is **WHAT** happens.

Let's start with the **WHO**, the hero of your story.

The Hero (the WHO)

The hero of a story is the main character. Usually it is the person we first meet and they are always the one whose story we follow. Another word for the hero is 'protagonist', which comes from Greek for the 'first competitor' and has the word 'battle' (*agon*) at its root.

In the beginning of storytelling, thousands of years before writing was invented, the hero was almost always a male warrior who was half god and half human.

Achilles from the Greek myths was a warrior who fought against the Trojans. He had a mortal father and a divine mother, the sea-nymph Thetis.

Achilles was faster, stronger and better-looking than ordinary humans, but he was still mortal like his father, which meant he could be killed.

When Achilles was a baby, his mother dipped him in magic waters that would protect him. But she held him by his heel and the magic water did not touch him there.

That place on Achilles' heel was his fatal weakness. One day his Trojan enemy Paris shot him there with a poisoned arrow and Achilles died. Even today we call someone's weakness their 'Achilles' heel', after the mythical Greek warrior.

Some writers call the hero's weakness their 'fatal flaw'.

It's always good to give a hero or superhero an Achilles' heel or weakness. Otherwise we know they'll win every battle and there will be no suspense.

Take Superman from the comic books. Like Achilles, he is invulnerable apart from one weakness: kryptonite! The creators of Superman knew it would be boring if he could easily win every battle against his enemy Lex Luthor.

The most interesting type of Achilles' heel is not a physical weakness, but a personality flaw. That is because many of us can identify with a hero's flaw and learn along with them. Sometimes we overcome our flaws. Sometimes we learn to live with them. The interesting thing about a personality flaw is that the flip side of a WEAKNESS is often a STRENGTH. For example, in the TV series *Sherlock*, Sherlock Holmes is tactless and often cruel in his dealings with other people, but that is a result of a quirky mind that makes him a genius. The Achilles' heel is more than a device to keep the story exciting. It's the thing that makes the hero human, so that – like us – they can learn to live a good life despite their flaws.

A hero doesn't have to be a man like Achilles, Superman or Sherlock Holmes. Your hero can be anyone. Your hero can be male or female, old or young, with superpowers or just ordinary. In fact your hero doesn't even have to be human. One of my favourite heroes is the little garbage robot called WALL-E from the 2008 Pixar film.

The hero of a story can even be a villain. In *Despicable Me*, the main character is Gru, an evil mastermind. Other movies that feature a 'villain' as the hero are *Megamind* and *Maleficent*. Those heroes are technically villains because they have really big flaws and want to do bad things. Sometimes we call a main character like this an 'antihero'.

Sometimes you get a hero who has no flaws; they are pretty much perfect. Some people call the perfect hero a **travelling angel**.

When I was a child I loved the Nancy Drew Mysteries, because Nancy is a hero who uses her head. She is a truth-seeker who wants justice. She would come upon a mystery, solve it and move on to the next. Nancy Drew is a good example of a travelling angel, a hero with no flaws.

Many years later when I was trying to be a writer, my sister said, 'Why don't you write a kids' book set in Pompeii?' The moment she said that I thought: *Nancy Drew in ancient Rome!* As soon as that thought popped into my head, I had a **cascade of ideas**. I knew what the series would be. Most importantly, I knew who the hero would be.

My main character would be a Roman girl who solved mysteries. I would call her Flavia Gemina. But unlike Nancy Drew, who is a kind of travelling angel, I would give her a flaw: the same flaw I have. I would make her bossy and impulsive. Essentially Flavia is a mixture of me and Nancy Drew. (That's a simple formula for your hero right there: you + your favourite fictional character = your hero.)

The flip side of Flavia's flaw (her impulsive bossiness) is that she is also decisive, confident and a good detective.

But her impulsiveness will get her into lots of trouble. And writers like trouble. We also like conflict. It keeps the reader interested and it helps the hero learn to live with their Achilles' heel.

Caroline's MIND MAP
THRESHOLD GUARDIANS
GUARD AGAINST EVIL
CROSSING THE THRESHOLD
HERO STEPS INTO New World
The HERO
The 5 CHARACTER ARCHETYPES
The MENTOR
The FAITHFUL SIDEKICK
The WILD ONE
The FUNNY ONE
John Truby's 7 PLOT BEATS
Stolen signet ring
1. PROBLEM
2. DESIRE
SPECIFIC and VISIBLE
Get the ring back
3. OPPONENT
4. THE PLAN
might involve:
training
collecting helpers
Lures magpie to nest

OPPOSITES
FLAW
GIFT
HeRO
TRAVELLING ANGEL
HOW to Write a GREAT STORY!
FOUR CHARACTERS
FLAVIA
LUPUS
JONATHAN
NUBIA
She is on a Higher Level
Learns that she's a good detective
7. NEW LEVEL
6. KNOWLEDGE
5. BATTLE
Into the woods
The Thieves of Ostia
The Secrets of Vesuvius
The Assassins of Rome
The Pirates of Pompeii

The Setting (the WHERE)

The setting is the place or places where your story happens. Settings are important. You need to establish it from the first paragraph, or your character is floating in black nothingness.

That doesn't mean you should open with a big chunk of description. Sometimes just a word or two will tell your reader when and where the story starts. You can then scatter in more details as the story goes along. (See **Ninja Description**).

However, you will need to know your setting intimately. Not just what your world looks like, but also what it sounds, smells and feels like. That's why you should choose a place and time you are familiar with. Or one you can easily imagine. Then you will need to describe it using all five senses.

Can't think of a setting? Try daydreaming one.

Daydream to Music

Put on a piece of music. Words distract the daydreaming part of our brain, so it's best to try music with no lyrics. When the music is on, close your eyes and use your imagination. Where does the music make you think of? A mountain top? City? Beach? Underwater? Outer space? An ancient temple? What time of day does the music suggest? What is the weather like? Is anybody in the scene? What are they doing? What do you smell and hear?

Try writing down what you saw and felt and smelled and heard before it fades.

Ignore the voice in your head telling you that it's a stupid exercise. Way back in 2002 I was on a creative-writing course. The teacher put on some sad violin music. At first I resisted, but when I gave in and let my imagination paint a scene, I suddenly 'saw' a funeral procession in the Roman port of Ostia on a foggy day. It wasn't clear, but still: there it was. Later that image became a scene in my thirteenth Roman Mystery, *The Slave-girl from Jerusalem*. When the BBC filmed some of my books to make a TV series, that scene featured in the opening-credits sequence.

It's strange, isn't it? A scene I almost refused to imagine ended up in the main titles of *The Roman Mysteries* TV series. That's the power of daydreaming.

The Plot (the WHAT)

Once you have your hero, you have to tell WHAT happens to them. You need a plot. The ancient Greek philosopher Aristotle wrote that every story has a beginning, middle and an end. But when I started writing, I found those three steps were too basic to help me plan my story.

Hollywood screenwriters know about plot structure. They have to get it right because movies cost millions of dollars to produce.

There are several different recipes for writing a plot, from Aaron Sorkin's two-step mantra of Intention and Obstacle to the **Hero's Journey**, which has between twelve and seventeen steps, depending on the version.

These different plot-structure formulas are not the Ten Commandments. They are not chiselled in stone. You can play around with them or even ignore them, but you should at least know what they are if you want to be an author or filmmaker.

The plot-structure formula that helped me get my first book published was a simple seven-step plot plan than I learned from a Hollywood script doctor named John Truby.

It's a great formula because it includes beginning, middle and end, but adds some really useful steps. But before I tell you about the seven steps, let me tell you a story.

In the first chapter of my first book, *The Thieves of Ostia*, I introduce my ten-year-old detective Flavia by having her solve a mini-mystery. Her father has a problem: his signet ring has gone missing. Because the ring is important to him, and because Flavia loves her dad, it's her problem too. Flavia looks for clues and finds a mark like an inky bird footprint on one of the documents her father was sealing. She spots the likely

culprit, a magpie, perching smugly in a tree in their inner garden. His beak is empty, which means if he did steal the ring then he probably took it to his nest. And now he's back for more!

Flavia devises a plan to get the magpie to lead her to his nest. She places a silver chain on her dad's desk in a beam of sunlight where it sparkles temptingly. The magpie takes the bait and flies off over the back wall of the house. Flavia runs to the back door, opens it and hesitates. Because her house is built into the town wall, one step over the threshold – the stone slab at the bottom of her door – will take her not just out of her home, but out of the whole town of Ostia.

Surrounding every Roman town is the graveyard, also known as the necropolis or 'city of the dead'. Flavia's dad has warned her never to go out there because it is full of danger: wild dogs, possible kidnappers and maybe evil spirits of the dead. But Flavia desperately wants to find her dad's ring, so she steps over the threshold and lets the door slam behind her. There is no door handle on the outside so she is locked out. There is no going back now! Trying not to let the magpie see her, she follows him through the woods.

For a terrible moment Flavia loses sight of his black and white feathers . . . but then she spies him popping up from an old oak tree. And his beak is empty! She waits until he flies away, runs to the tree and climbs it. Eureka! Flavia finds her dad's stolen ring and has a revelation: she is a good detective! She also finds a gold and emerald earring with dangly pearls that she will sell to the goldsmith for six gold coins. With that money she buys a beautiful slave girl called Nubia, to save her from a terrible fate.

That example, the first chapter of my first book, illustrates **Truby's Seven Plot Beats**, from his book, *The Anatomy of Story: 22 Steps to Becoming A Master Storyteller,* that help create a great story and also a good scene or chapter.

1. Problem (Need)

Every story starts with a problem. Some heroes have massive problems. In James Bond movies, an evil mastermind often wants to destroy the world. In *The Very Hungry Caterpillar* a caterpillar is very hungry. Flavia's problem is that her dad has lost his signet ring. This is not an earth-shaking problem but

it's a problem. The Need, in brackets, is the thing the hero needs to learn to live a better life and is often related to their Achilles' heel.

2. Desire

The hero wants something that will solve their problem. When you really want something, you desire it. This is the engine of your story. The desire can be for a magic sword, a beautiful princess, or world peace. The best desires are often things you can see and hold so you know when you've obtained them. If your hero has a desire that can't be seen, it's good to have a symbol of the desire. In the 2014 movie

Paddington, Paddington's problem is that his jungle home is gone. His desire is to go to London, 'where he will be assured of a warm welcome'. This desire is symbolised by the brief glimpse of a London snow globe. Flavia's desire is clear and tangible: she wants her dad's stolen ring.

3. Opponent

The opponent can be evil, like a James Bond villain, but they don't always have to be bad. They are just someone or something that clashes with your hero as they go after their desire. In Flavia's search for her dad's ring, the magpie is her opponent. But he isn't evil; he just likes bright shiny things. In our own lives, our opponents – the people we clash with – are often our friends and family! Sometimes, instead of a living opponent you get an inanimate object: inner fear, distance to be travelled timescale to accomplish the desire. The outer opponent is often the perfect person to challenge the hero's deeper need.

4. PLAN

I put the PLAN in capital letters because it takes up the middle of a story. This step often includes a journey, training and the collection of helpers. It almost always involves the hero crossing a threshold into a new world. In a short story the hero's plan works immediately. In a longer story the opponent may thwart the hero's plan or come up with a plan of his own, and lots of other things can go wrong.

5. Battle

The beginning of the end is often a battle. It doesn't have to be a literal battle with swords or guns or flame-throwers. It can be a courtroom scene or a debate. It can be a competition. In a love story the battle could be a boy and girl having an argument in the back of a taxi. Flavia's battle is with the magpie. If she finds his nest and recovers the

treasure, *she* wins the battle. If he keeps his nest a secret and gets to keep his sparkly things then *he* wins the battle. In fact, the opponent might not even know they are in a battle.

6. Knowledge (Reward)

The real point of every scene is that your hero learns something they need to know. The Reward (in brackets) is what they wanted, their desire. Almost always, it is better for them to learn something useful than to get the desire. If they get the desire *and* learn something useful, it is a win-win situation. In the story of the missing signet ring, Flavia doesn't just recover the ring, she realises something important about herself: that she's a good detective. If the hero doesn't get the desire and doesn't learn anything – or learns too late – it is a tragedy.

7. New Level

The new level is just another way of talking about a sad or happy outcome of the scene or story. It is like the lungs of your story. This step keeps your narrative breathing and moving. At the beginning of the first chapter of my first book, Flavia has a problem. Near the end of the chapter she solves it and is on a higher level. Straightaway I give her a new problem which brings her even lower than when she started: I end the chapter with wild dogs surrounding the tree with the magpie's nest. That's called a **cliffhanger**, and it keeps the reader reading or the watcher watching. Usually if your scene starts with the hero high, they will end lower, or if they start low they will end higher. But as in this scene you can start low and end even lower!

Those seven steps don't just provide structure for a whole book, they are often the structure of every scene.

Think of them as a recipe, or a road map. Once you write them down you don't have to slavishly obey them. They are simply guidelines. They can be changed or rewritten. They keep you on track.

Here are the seven plot beats again, in summary:

1. **Problem (Need)** – Your hero has a problem.

2. **Desire** – Your hero sees something they think will solve their problem.

3. **Opponent** - Someone or something also wants the object of desire and clashes with your hero as they go for it.

4. **PLAN** - The hero's plan to get their desire often involves a journey.

5. **Battle** - This is the final confrontation that decides whether the hero gets the object of desire.

6. **Knowledge (Reward)** - Whether your hero gets the thing they wanted or not, they learn something.

7. **New Level** - The hero is either better off or worse off than when they started.

I first began using this structure as a framework for my ideas, but over the years I realised the beauty of these seven steps is that we play them out every day of our lives. We all have our little desires and battles in the family: to use the bathroom first, have the last piece of toast, find our gym kit, check our device, etc. At school we have desires and battles too: avoid the bully, find our friend, get a good mark on the test, win the match, get the part we want in the school play, etc. We also have long-term desires: to get into a certain school, have a good career, make a difference in the world, start a family, etc. The seven steps show us that you can learn from every battle, whether or not you get the thing you desired.

HOW to REMEMBER TRUBY'S SEVEN PLOT BEATS USING the NUMBER-SHAPE System

beginning

1.  arrow — PROBLEM (Need)

2.  crystal swan — DESIRE

3.  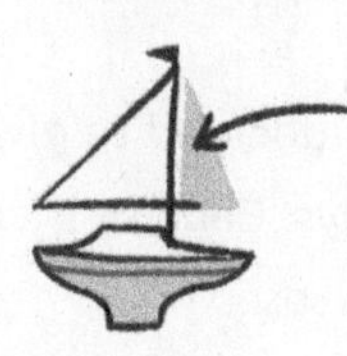 baby's bottom — OPPONENT

middle

4. yacht's sail — THE PLAN (Journey)

end

5.  five fingers — BATTLE!

6.  trunk — KNOWLEDGE

7.  cliff — NEW LEVEL

SIDEKICKS AND MENTORS

A few rare stories have just a hero on their own, often against the elements. One example is the classic short story by Hemingway *The Old Man and the Sea*. A rare example of a movie with only one character is *All Is Lost* about a sailor at sea whose boat has been damaged.

In most stories the hero has friends and helpers, or at the very least a sidekick. And each would embody one of the four elements: earth, air, fire and water. Sherlock Holmes has Dr Watson. Shrek has Donkey. Batman has Robin.

For my Roman Mysteries books, I decided to give Flavia three friends, one girl and two boys. Each of them would have their own skills and weaknesses.

I got this idea when I thought about some of my favourite movies and I realised that the hero often has three main sidekicks or helpers.

Take *The Wizard of Oz*, *Star Wars*, Pixar's *Up*, *The Lord of the Rings* and Harry Potter. They all have a hero with more or less three sidekicks.

The Faithful Sidekick

Dorothy's animal sidekick is Toto, but of the three characters she meets on the Yellow Brick Road she grows closest to Scarecrow. Mr Carl Frederickson's faithful sidekick is Russell the Junior Wilderness Explorer. Luke has R2-D2, as faithful as any dog. Frodo has Sam. Harry Potter has Ron Weasley. In my Roman Mysteries, Nubia takes this role.

I call this character the 'faithful sidekick', because they are always faithful and loyal to the hero. Their skills usually complement the hero's skills, so the two of them make a good team. Because the faithful sidekick really cares about the hero, they often challenge the hero's behaviour. In many stories, the faithful sidekick saves the hero's life or brings them back from death. In some stories, the faithful sidekick is even prepared to die for the hero.

The Funny One

In dangerous and exciting stories, you need to laugh to release tension. One of my favourite sidekick characters is what I call the 'funny one'. In *Star Wars*, George Lucas introduced the robot C-3PO to add comic relief. I often wonder if he got the idea from the Tin Man in *The Wizard of Oz*. In Pixar's *Up*, Doug the dog is very funny. In my Roman Mysteries books, Flavia's next-door neighbour Jonathan fills this role. Sometimes the funny one is two people, like Pippin and Merry in *The Lord of the Rings*. Sometimes the funny one is the same as the faithful sidekick, like Ron Weasley. You can mix and match.

The Wild One

Often, as the hero goes on the journey to get the desire and solve the problem, someone appears who seems to be an opponent, but then turns out to be a helper. Think of the Cowardly Lion when he first jumps out of the bushes and roars. Dorothy and her other new friends are frightened, until they discover he's a big softie and learn to like him. Or think of Robin Hood when he meets Little John on a log bridge. At first they fight but then they become friends. This character is often like an animal in certain ways so I call them the 'wild one'. In *Star Wars*, the wild one is Chewbacca, who is a kind of cowardly lion. In Pixar's *Up*, a big bird called Kevin scares us at first, until we realise *she* wants to get home to her babies! In my Roman Mysteries, Lupus the mute beggar boy is the wild one.

Watching movies and re-reading my favourite Greek myths, I noticed a fifth character who often appears in great stories.

The Mentor

The mentor is often a wise wizard who appears early in the story and says to the hero, 'You must go on a quest to get the prize.' The hero doubts himself but the mentor encourages him. 'You can do it!' he says. 'I'll teach you and help you.' The mentor almost always gives the hero an object of special value, often with magical properties, to help him on the journey. This object is called a **talisman**.

In many stories the mentor is a wise old wizard with a beard and robes.

But the mentor doesn't have to be a man with a beard. In the myth of Theseus, the hero's mentor is his mother, Aethra. She tells Theseus that when he is strong enough to lift a massive rock he can go on a journey to seek his fortune. When Theseus is sixteen he finally lifts the rock and finds his father's sword underneath. That is his talisman.

In the 1939 movie *The Wizard of Oz*, the mentor is Glinda, the Good Witch of the North. She tells Dorothy to 'follow the yellow brick road' and she gives her a talisman: ruby slippers. In the first Percy Jackson book, Chiron gives Percy a pen that turns into a sword. In *Star Wars*, Obi-Wan gives Luke his father's lightsaber. Gandalf gives Frodo the One Ring, one of the most famous talismans in modern literature.

The Funny One

The 5 Character Archetypes

The Wild One

The HERO (ine)
The MENTOR
The FAITHFUL Sidekick

Because the mentor is essentially a teacher, there is a point where the pupil must 'graduate' and travel on their own to show what they have learned. This is why the mentor often dies or disappears around three-quarters of the way through a story. In a few instances they appear near the end to give the hero one last bit of help and also to congratulate them on finishing the quest.

Some mentors are unreliable (you might call them 'anti-mentors'), and sometimes the mentor can even be an opponent, putting his desires over those of the hero.

Archetypal Characters

These five characters - the hero, the faithful sidekick, the funny one, the wild one and the mentor - appear in thousands of movies and books. Although I made up some of the terms (like the funny one and the wild one), all writers know about them, even if they call them by different names. We call them 'archetypes', which means 'ancient model', because they go all the way back to ancient mythology.

These archetypal characters are just as powerful in books and movies today as they were when we were cavemen sitting around a fire.

Just because these types are ancient doesn't mean you can't make them fresh and modern.

THE JOURNEY

A big part of many stories is the journey. To defeat the opponent and get the desire, the hero must go on a quest. The mentor usually sends the hero on this journey and sidekicks are collected on the way. In Truby's seven-step story structure, this main journey usually occurs in the middle step, the plan. This journey almost always includes a step called **crossing the threshold**.

The best kind of journey takes the hero from their **ordinary world** into the **world of adventure**, whether it's Frodo stepping outside his hobbit hole or Luke Skywalker zooming away from his desert planet into the stars.

Remember Achilles, the hero with the vulnerable heel? He was one of the Greeks who fought the Trojans. The Trojans had heroes too. One of them was called Aeneas. Like Achilles, he had a mortal father and a divine mother. Aeneas's mother was Venus, the goddess of love. Aeneas is one of my favourite examples of a hero who goes on a journey.

Aeneas's Problem

The Greeks besieged the citadel of Troy for ten years and only defeated their enemy by means of a trick. They pretended to sail away, leaving a giant wooden horse on the beach as an offering to the gods. The Trojans brought the horse inside the city walls (across the threshold!) and celebrated their victory over the Greeks. But that night a secret door in the horse opened up and Greek soldiers dropped out. They opened the gate to let the other Greeks in. Then they set Troy on fire and began to kill as many people as possible.

According to the story as told by the Latin poet Virgil, Aeneas wants to stay and fight the Greeks, but his mother Venus appears to him in the role of mentor and tells him to take his family and get out. Aeneas has to take his son and elderly father, and their household gods as a talisman. He crosses a threshold when he goes through the city gate and leaves the danger of burning Troy for the safety of dark and magical woods.

With the help of other refugees from Troy, Aeneas uses the special trees of the forest to build boats. Soon they cross another threshold when they set off across the sea to find a new homeland, a 'New Troy'.

Aeneas's Journey to the Underworld

In Greek myths and epics there can be several journeys within the quest. One of these journeys is often to the underworld, also known as Hades.

Hercules' final labour is to fetch Cerberus the three-headed hellhound from Hades. The hero musician Orpheus must go to Hades to bring back his wife Eurydice.

Aeneas has to go to the underworld too. His mentor for this

journey is a prophetess called the Sybil, and his talisman is a golden branch of mistletoe. Rivers often act as thresholds and Aeneas must cross the River Styx which divides the land of the living from the land of the dead. He must also get past a **threshold guardian**: Cerberus, the three-headed hound.

Paddington's Problem

In the 2014 movie *Paddington*, our young hero is a lot like Aeneas. Paddington Bear has lost his home and some of his family. He must go on a journey to find a new homeland. His mentor is his Aunt Lucy and the talisman is his Uncle Pastuzo's hat. Not only does the hat give Paddington confidence, but it reminds him of his past and will help him find his desire. (Plus it contains a marmalade sandwich for emergencies.)

Like many heroes, Paddington must cross the threshold alone. He steps into the lifeboat on a massive container boat and then travels to London, over ten thousand kilometres away. But the makers of the film didn't just have one crossing the threshold; because it's such a fun step, they gave him about five or six.

When Paddington gets to London and meets the Brown family he wants to live with them. Do you remember the moment where Paddington gets out of the taxi and goes to the Browns' front door? We are shown his wet little paws stepping over a *literal* threshold, the bar at the bottom of a doorway. This is because Paddington's desire is to live in that house with the Browns.

Later, in Mr Gruber's shop, Paddington watches a film of his home in Peru and, like *Alice Through the Looking Glass* he magically steps through the screen and into his memories for one last glimpse of his childhood home.

Paddington's Journey to the Underworld

Paddington makes a kind of journey to the underworld when he finds himself at the top of an escalator in the London Underground. He is afraid to take that first step onto the moving stairs until he sees a sign saying 'Dogs Must Be Carried'. Paddington's misunderstanding of the sign makes for a very funny scene. The sign was a kind of mentor to Paddington, giving him encouragement, and the cute little dog is his talisman. It gives him confidence. You can see how the story of an ancient Greek hero, first told over two thousand years ago, and the story of a talking bear from Peru hit many of the same beats. And both are examples of superb storytelling.

WRITING ON THE RIGHT SIDE OF THE BRAIN

One of the books that changed my life is a book called *Drawing on the Right Side of the Brain*. The author, Betty

Edwards, says that when you draw what you SEE not what you KNOW, you go quiet and find it hard to talk because you've made a mental shift from the logical left side of the brain to the creative right side of the brain.

I believe this is why it's so hard for writers to sit down and start writing. You'd think the left brain would love it. After all, writing is a bunch of words, and the left brain loves words. But writing is using those words to make vivid pictures with colour, movement, emotion and the senses. The left brain has to let the right brain play . . . and it is always resistant to that.

You have to keep telling your logical, verbal, critical left brain not to worry. 'Play nicely with your other half! I still love you. You are vital to me. I couldn't live without you. But you know you're better when you work together!'

One and one is usually two. But when you put your left brain together with your right brain, you get a bazillion!

I used to do lots of tutoring and one of the skills I taught was how to use special memory techniques. Several books had shown me that the best way to memorise a list of names or dates is to link the items with fun, colourful, moving images.

One way of remembering items in a list is to use the number-shape memory system where each number suggests an object that you link with another image representing the thing you want to remember.

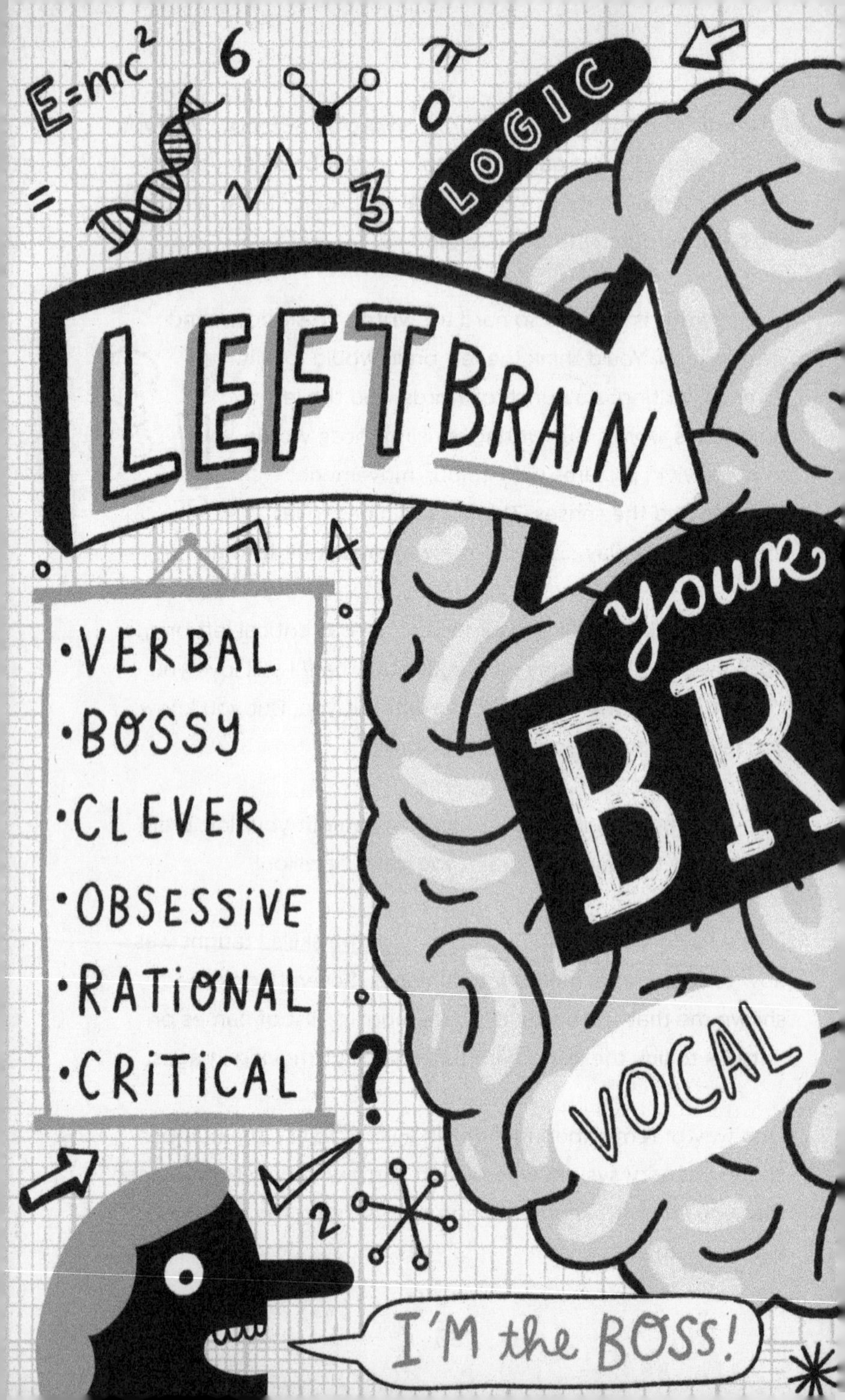
E=mc²
6
0
3
LOGIC
LEFT BRAIN
4
• VERBAL
• BOSSY
• CLEVER
• OBSESSIVE
• RATIONAL
• CRITICAL
?
2
your
BR
VOCAL
I'M the BOSS!

VISUAL
ART
Music
SPORTS
AIN
Right BRAIN
DAYDREAMS
CREATIVITY

Can you see how the number one could be represented by a standing up arrow?

Close your eyes and see if you can imagine that arrow. Imagine reaching out to touch the shaft. Is it wood or metal? You choose. Your brain is in control. Imagine how smooth it is under your fingertips, like a round pencil. Now imagine stroking the feathers. What colour are the feathers? Now imagine going back up the shaft to the arrowhead, the tip. Ouch! Now imagine someone taking that arrow, notching it in a bow, pulling back the bow string and aiming it at you! You would have a problem.

You can apply this technique to learning Truby's seven beats.

1 = arrow = (someone aiming arrow) = **Problem**

2 = swan = (imagine a crystal swan) = **Desire**

3 = baby's bottom (if turned on side) = **Opponent**

4 = sail of a yacht = **PLAN** (often includes a journey)

5 = five fingers (make a fist and punch) = **Battle**

6 = elephant trunk = (elephants never forget) = **Knowledge**

7 = cliff = **New Level** (often a 'cliffhanger')

The principle of using both sides of your brain comes up again and again in creative writing. That's why I do memory exercises like this in my writing classes: to illustrate how powerful our brains are when we link the logical left brain and the creative right brain.

Structure Is a Road Map

When it came to writing my second book, I thought, *I don't need to plot this one out; I know how to write now*. I was wrong! That second book was one of the hardest books I've ever written. I realised how much I needed my steps to keep me heading in the right direction. So now I always plot out the main beats, whether I'm using Truby's seven beats, **the hero's journey**, **Save the Cat** or a mixture of the three. Then I write my **chapter outline**. My structure beats often change, but I still know where I'm heading. In between all that left brain structure, I use my right brain by daydreaming, putting on music and going for walks. Most of all, I try to remember to **have fun!**

How to Write YOUR Story

The most important thing you can ever learn is What You Are Meant To Do In This Life. It won't just be one thing; it will be many things. In order to discover what you're good at doing, sometimes you need to discover the things you're not so good at doing.

That's why you go to school every day to do battle with your teachers, friends and rivals. You do it to figure out your likes and dislikes, your strengths and your weaknesses.

That's why your best hero is one based on you. Because as your hero learns, so will you.

This is the approach I have taken for many – but not all – of my books. It is also the approach I take when I do workshops in schools. It means we come up with a plot outline that is relevant to the group I'm guiding.

The following three sample workshops are based on writing workshops I have done in schools or with grown-up friends. You can do them as a group or on your own. You choose.

SAMPLE WORKSHOP #1

Start with the Achilles' Heel

Start off with your hero's flaw but make it relevant to you. What is your hero's Achilles' heel, the thing that gets them in trouble? In school workshops, I ask kids to suggest their own weaknesses. What is the thing you know gets you in trouble but you just can't master? I start by confessing mine:

my impatience. Here are a few we often come up with: hot-tempered, nosy, lazy, bossy, chatterbox, too shy to speak, too eager to please, easily tempted, etc.

The beauty of the Achilles' heel is that there is often a flip side, like on a coin. Someone who is hot-tempered might also be very brave. Someone who is nosy might make a good detective. Someone who is a chatterbox might become a great lawyer, whereas someone who hates speaking might be good at listening and make a brilliant counsellor. When the hero learns how to live with their Achilles' heel, or overcome it and make it work for them, that is always a valuable lesson for all of us too. Especially if we share that flaw.

A few years ago I was writer-in-residence at a school in London and I did this exercise with pupils in Years Four and Five (aged 8–10).

In sessions of about an hour, I quickly introduced the seven plot beats and the Achilles' heel. Then we brainstormed a story. We started by choosing a weakness that many of us could identify with – an Achilles' heel. In each group we made a list and then voted for our favourite. Once we had the weakness, we named the hero and chose details about them to fit that weakness. Then we figured out What They Would Learn (step 6, the knowledge), who their best opponent would be (step 3) and the best arena for the battle (step 5). Still brainstorming, we chose the best problem (step 1) and desire (step 2) to bring our hero into the battle so that they could get the knowledge. We thought about the middle of the story, where the hero has to come up with a plan to defeat the opponent to get the desire to solve the problem and also get the knowledge that will satisfy the need. In some sessions we even had time to add a mentor and a journey to step 4, the plan. Finally, we decided which new level our hero would end up on: higher or lower. I wrote out all the steps on the board with little arrows and notes as we came up with ideas. Some we kept, some were crossed out after we voted.

Notice that if you start with the Achilles' heel and the knowledge, you might not even come up with the problem until late in the planning. It starts every scene or story, but it doesn't always start the planning process.

Here are the some of the **elevator pitches** we ended up with.

'A Saucepan Saved My Life' (Achilles' heel = Nosy)
Bobetta is naturally nosy and wants to become a reporter on the school newspaper. September, the snooty editor of the paper, will only let her join the staff if she first writes a profile on the new chef at school, a Frenchman named Georges. While investigating the new cook, Bobetta makes a horrifying discovery: Georges is a murderer who likes to poison people en masse! The battle takes place in the kitchen and cafeteria and ends with a massive food fight.

'The Trophy' (Achilles' heel = Terrified of Speaking in Public)
Tina knows she is the best poet in the school, but to win the valuable Poetry Trophy she must read her poem out loud to the whole school. And nothing terrifies her more than public speaking. Will her super-confident rival Priscilla take the prize with an inferior poem?

'Vanessa Chatbag: The Girl Who Wouldn't Stop Talking' (Achilles' heel = Chatterbox)
Vanessa's parents are very strict and never allow sweets or fizzy drinks, so she really wants her house to win The Feast (a special treat where junk food IS allowed). But she can't stop talking, and if she gets one more 'minus' in class, her house will lose. Her grandmother had the same problem as a girl, and advises Vanessa to tape her mouth shut. But Grandma Chatbag's advice fails spectacularly and Vanessa gets TWO minuses! What can she do now?

'Bossyboots' (Achilles' heel = Too Bossy)
Erica's parents have promised her the holiday of a lifetime if she can win her school's Conduct Cup. But Erica is incredibly bossy and can't stop clashing with her teacher, Mrs Higgins. She manages to get some good advice from her best friend Nancy, but when a crisis occurs in the final assembly of the year Erica learns that sometimes being bossy can save lives!

SAMPLE WORKSHOP #2

Start with the Setting

I did a very similar workshop at a secondary school, where we started by brainstorming the Achilles' heel. But this time, we added a preliminary step. We started with the setting: ancient Rome.

This was the order in which we 'beat it out'.

1. The setting
2. The hero's Achilles' heel
3. The hero's knowledge (what they will learn)
4. The hero's gender
5. The hero's name
6. The hero's opponent
7. The arena for the battle
8. The hero's problem and desire
9. The hero's plan, including possible friends plus a mentor and a talisman
10. The hero's new level at the end of the story
11. The elevator pitch
12. A working title

In addition to many of the usual flaws, such as being impatient, lazy and moody, here are some more unusual Achilles' heels the students came up with: selfish, insecure, overly confident, lacks empathy, jealous of sibling, obsessive about dirt, can't keep secrets.

Here are some of the brilliant elevator pitches we came up with after an hour or so of brainstorming, discussion and voting as we worked through the steps above. See if you can guess the hero's Achilles' heel in each case.

'The Praetorian Slave'
In the age of Nero, an arrogant Praetorian guard named Maximus is wrongly accused of treason and sent to be a slave at Monte Testaccio, a hill of broken pottery where slaves break up used amphoras and sprinkle them with caustic lime powder. In this ancient hell on earth he is befriended by another slave and learns to put himself in other people's sandals. The oldest slave on the hill, now blind from years of exposure to lime powder, tells them how to get out. But when they try to escape, things go wrong and Maximus must make the hardest decision of his life.

'Gemini' or 'The Jealous Sister'
In the age of Julius Caesar, Scintilla longs for the freedom and power enjoyed by her twin brother, Gaius. Her plan is to disguise herself as Gaius, but then she meets Cleopatra, who will teach her how a woman can be powerful in the man's world of the Roman Republic.

'Saving Roma'
It is the year AD *409. The Emperor Honorius has a pet chicken he calls Roma, whom he loves more than his own subjects. When an overly confident Roman girl named Julia follows the chicken-loving Emperor Honorius to Ravenna in order to tell him that Rome is in danger from invading Germans, she makes a journey that will change her life forever.*

'Atlas'
Atlas, a brave gladiator from Mauretania, dreams of winning the rudus, *the wooden sword of freedom. But dirt disgusts him and he is compelled to wash obsessively. One day, in Nero's Rome, he has the chance to be free, but only if he can overcome his fear and go into Rome's sewers, the Cloaca Maxima.*

'Journey to Jerusalem'
Ruben can't keep secrets and one day his rash words cause the death of a group of Christian worshippers at the hands of his father, an imperial enforcer. Ruben has to journey to Jerusalem to atone for his crime.

As a follow-up exercise, I asked the students to write the first paragraph in the style of their favourite author. The results were brilliant with kids imitating J. K. Rowling, J. D. Salinger and Rick Riordan (who may have been influenced by Salinger's style, we noticed!). One boy even wrote four stanzas of *The Praetorian Slave* in the style of Dr Seuss! It was genius.

SAMPLE WORKSHOP #3

Start with a Title and a First Line

Another great way to start a story is with a title and some first lines.

At another primary school I asked the students to bring a favourite book, writing paper and pens. I began by appointing myself head writer in a **writers' room** in which the pupils were my team of writers. I chose the title – 'Escape from Vesuvius' – and reasoned that as there were thousands of people in the town of Pompeii when Vesuvius erupted, there must have been thousands of stories, each one different.

Because the title had been assigned by me, we started with first lines. I encouraged students to read out some of the first lines from their books. Using those first lines as inspiration, we chopped and changed a few words and names to make them Roman. That gave us not only our story but our hero too.

The line that started us all off was the first sentence of *The Hobbit*: 'In a hole in the ground there lived a hobbit.'

Instead of a hobbit we decided it should be a runaway slave. When I took a vote on whether our hero should be a boy or a girl, the class was split. So I suggested one of my favourite tropes, a girl dressed as a boy or vice versa. We decided to make it a boy who would dress as a girl when the volcano erupted. That could be part of his plan to escape. Instead of a hole in the ground, we put him in a hole in a house abandoned in the earthquake a few years before the eruption. By now we had changed 'hole in the ground' to 'the ruins of a house destroyed by an earthquake' so that nothing was left of the original sentence.

We got an idea that our runaway slave would have four pets from the first line of *Peter Rabbit*: 'Once upon a time there were four little Rabbits, and their names were Flopsy, Mopsy, Cotton-tail, and Peter.' We changed the rabbits to mice, and one boy suggested naming them after Roman emperors. So now we had our hero's sidekicks! (The fact that our hero has made vermin his pets also tells us he is kind.) We also realised that, for this one boy, the volcano might be a good thing because in the confusion he can run away. But because it's often best to have a human opponent we came up with the obvious one: his master.

This was the elevator pitch:

'Escape from Vesuvius'
Dictys is a runaway slave who lives in the ruins of a Pompeiian house damaged by the earthquake seventeen years before. His only companions are four mice whom he has named Caligula, Nero, Augustus and Claudius. When Vesuvius suddenly erupts,

what will be a disaster for thousands might be his one chance for freedom! Dictys decides he will have a better chance at escape if he dresses as a girl, just in case he runs into his cruel former master.

Our new first line was: *'Master,' squeaked Caligula, 'the volcano is erupting!'*

Everyone loved the approach of starting from a favourite first line because it meant that each person could use a book and style of writing that appealed to them as their source of inspiration. (See **Finding Your Voice**.)

DAILY ROUTINE

I know a few brilliant writers, like Geraldine McCaughrean and Anthony Horowitz, who love writing and spend every free minute doing it, but personally I need to force myself to sit down and write. Otherwise I'd spend all day reading, going to movies and meeting friends. Most authors have a daily routine of some sort to make sure they put in the hours. After all, one of the best (and worst!) things about being a writer is that you are your own boss. My routine has changed over the years according to my age and circumstances, but one of the constants has been that I do almost all my writing in the morning, leaving the afternoon for research and relaxation.

(The bossy left brain is better in the morning but then it gets tired, so the dreamy right brain often takes over in the afternoon). At the moment my daily routine goes a bit like this: I get up some time between 5.30 and 7.30 a.m. Usually my mind is fizzing with ideas that have come to me in my sleep.

I do twenty minutes' yoga and finish with ten minutes of prayer and meditation. (This is when more good ideas often pop into my head.)

Then I sit at my computer and try to write uninterrupted for three or four hours. I don't usually have breakfast until after I've put in at least two hours. That means I don't eat until between 9 a.m. and 11 a.m. I try to eat vegetables, protein and good fats like nuts, eggs, avocado or last night's warmed-up chili con carne, because carbohydrates (bread, croissants, sugar, etc) make me sleepy and hungry.

A few writers can work anywhere, e.g. in any room of the house, in a cafe, on a train or even a bus. But I write best in my study with my computer, books and files around me.

Around midday I have lunch – usually a salad or steamed broccoli with mayonnaise (which I love).

In the afternoon I go out to a movie, a museum or to meet a friend, sometimes for a **writers' date**. Sometimes I just take a walk in the park or along the riverside.

I try to walk at least two miles a day, which isn't difficult as I don't have a car. Whenever I am walking or taking public transport, I listen to music, podcasts and audiobooks. I get lots of inspiration and ideas from those.

Around 4 p.m. I have a twenty-minute 'power nap'. I have a selection of slow songs that put me into a light sleep and then an upbeat one that brings me back. I use my right brain to imagine where the music is taking me, so even if I don't sleep, I am hugely refreshed.

My husband Richard makes dinner and because I grew up in California we eat the American way, around 6 p.m. watching some of our favourite TV shows, anything from *Young Sheldon* to *The Crown*. After dinner I do a bit more admin: emailing schools in preparation for author visits, buying train tickets and making up invoices. I never listen to music when I write, but I often do while I'm doing these chores.

After that my husband Richard and I watch one more TV show.

Then bath and bed between 11 p.m. and midnight. I read in bed but get sleepy very quickly. Sometimes I wake up in the middle of the night with an idea and I jot it down in the **writer's notebook** I keep beside my bed.

That was my routine when I was writing this book, but I am always ready to adapt to new circumstances. In the same way, you need to find what works for you.

Caroline's DAY:
The WRITER'S way

05:30
GET UP
IDEAS
BRAIN FIZZING!

30 mins of YOGA and PRAYERFUL MEDITATION

6:45 am

10 am
BREAKfast
NUTS.

10:30
TAP
TAP
TAP

NOON
LUNCH
Healthy Salad

1pm
WALK in NATURE

POWER NAP
ZZzzz
4pm

6pm

WORK ADMIN
7pm
INVOICE

11pm

00:00
Writer's NOTEBOOK
Good Night!

YOUR STORY COULD CHANGE THE WORLD

'We as writers are the new lawmakers, the new prophets . . . if we choose to be.'

John Truby

Sometimes a miraculous thing happens.

You have an idea in your head, a **light bulb moment**.

Then you work it through: on paper a little, on computer a bit, but still mostly in your head, talking to yourself, imagining scenes, pitting characters against each other. You keep refilling your creative refrigerator by reading, walking, listening to music, eavesdropping on conversations, going to movies, watching TV . . . Then more writing and a little rewriting.

And then, one day, people read it. Or maybe even watch it. They like it. They dream about it. They think about the characters. They talk about it with their friends and families. Sometimes a book, movie or TV show can spark an interest that changes someone's life or inspires their career. And it all started as an idea in your head.

your STORY can CHANGE the WORLD

Some stories even become part of the culture. Most teachers in your school would understand if you said, 'The game is afoot!' or, 'May the Force be with you,' or, 'I'm a Hufflepuff.'

These stories become 'universes', like the 'Marvel Universe', or franchises like *The Hunger Games*. People produce little action figures or Lego figurines so that you can act out more scenarios of those stories. People dress up as the characters and go to conventions, all about a story that started in someone's head. It's crazy.

Sometimes a girl crying alone in her bedroom will console herself with thoughts of Katniss from *The Hunger Games*. Sometimes a boy will think twice about teasing someone with a disability because he's just seen the movie *Wonder*. Sometimes an office worker on a tube train will be thinking more about the story they're reading than about the finance meeting at 10.30.

Recently, a scholar named Yuval Noah Harari shared an interesting theory. He thinks the reason that *homo sapiens* (i.e. human beings) became the dominant animal on earth is because of our ability to make up stories and to believe them.

Stories are incredibly powerful, so if you become a writer, be careful!

Your story could change the world.

Caroline Lawrence, London, 2019

cool!
STORIES
YES!
STAR
OK
PART TWO

Achilles' Heel

Named after the mythical Greek hero Achilles, this is a term for a character's weakness, often one that can be used by their opponent to try to defeat them. Giving your hero an Achilles' heel is great way into your story. It's often the first thing I start with. The 2016 movie *Sing* has six heroes, each of whom has an Achilles' heel which they need to overcome. Max the koala is unrealistically optimistic, Rosita the pig is distracted by her twenty-five piglets, Mike the mouse is arrogant and over-confident, Ash the punk hedgehog is depressed following a break-up, Johnny the gorilla was raised to be a criminal and Meena the hippo suffers crippling stage fright. By the end of the film each of them learns to overcome their weakness so that they can SING!

ARC

This is a term used by writers and reviewers to describe the development of the character or the plot (Also known as a **character arc**) . One of the most popular teachers of screenwriting, Blake Snyder, says that stories are 'change machines'. He talks about the **opening image** and the **closing image** – in comparing these we can clearly see how much a character has changed over the course of a story. The hero starts in their ordinary life, but by undergoing tests, trials and battles they finish by achieving their potential to be extraordinary. In *Star Wars*, Luke doubts his own abilities but by the end he is a Jedi warrior who can use the Force. The main characters from *The Matrix*, Harry Potter and *Wonder* also end by realising their potential. If the hero is a **travelling angel** they don't need to change, but we see how they change the world around them. Paul King, writer/director of the Paddington movies, once old me that in *Paddington 2* our furry hero questions the principles of honesty and kindness that Aunt Lucy taught him, but by the end he has tested and confirmed their value.

Sometimes the hero's arc brings them to a lower level, but that can be satisfying for the audience too. We call it 'tragedy'.

THE ARENA

The word 'arena' comes from the Latin word for sand, *harena*, and originally meant a place where gladiators fought. It has since come to mean any place where a struggle or contest takes place. In myth and screenwriting, the hero often goes down to the underworld to fight the opponent, or up to a mountaintop. In modern superhero films the arena is often an entire city or even a whole planet. You could choose a famous monument for the **battle** (climax) of your story, like the Natural History Museum in *Paddington* or the Colosseum for *Gladiator* (the original arena). You could go up high, like Mr Carl Fredericksen and Russell in *UP*, who do battle on a blimp way up high. You could go down low, like Luke when he goes into the Death Star or WALL-E when he goes down to the garbage compactor on board the spaceship *Axiom*. The arena can also be somewhere ordinary like a car, a train, a boat or a room.

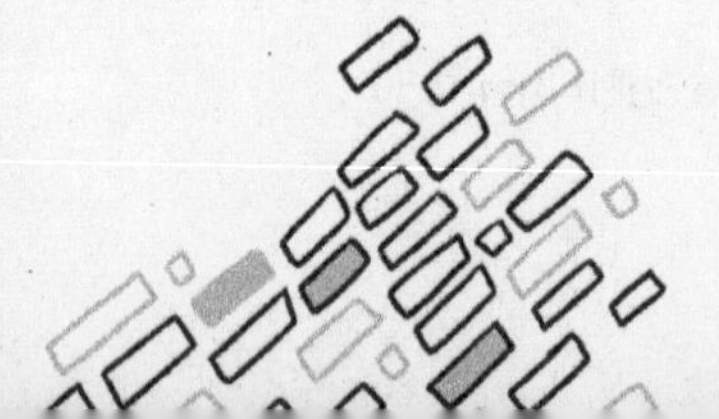

ARTEFACTS

People often ask me where I get my ideas. One answer is from artefacts. The word is Latin and means 'made by skill'. An artefact is something man-made. Many artefacts have inspired entire stories. For example, my *Time Travel Diaries* was partly inspired by an exotic ivory-and-iron clasp knife, whose handle was carved to resemble a leopard. It was buried with a fourteen-year-old Roman girl so must have been very precious to her. But why? I wrote the book partly to come up with a possible solution. Artefacts bring your world alive, and they are especially valuable in the genre of mystery stories, where a detective must search for clues. The artefact can become the hero's talisman too, as in my Roman Mysteries, where mute Lupus is very dependent on his wax-coated wooden writing tablet.

THE ARTIST'S DATE

In her inspirational book *The Artist's Way*, screenwriter Julia Cameron gives tips for unblocking your imagination and learning how to be creative. One tip I have found especially fun is the artist's date. Instead of going out with another person, you take your 'creative self' on a date. Going somewhere on your own allows you to set your own pace and focus completely on the art. You can go to a museum, art gallery, music concert or movie. It can be a free activity like taking a sketchbook to a park, cloud watching, or window-shopping in a creative place such as a music store or a craft shop. You can even have an artist's date in your bedroom. Go through old photo albums, dance barefoot to drum music for five minutes, sketch your sleeping pet, light incense and sit quietly for twenty minutes or rearrange your toys in a way that tells a story. However, like the hero of a story, it's often more powerful to leave your **ordinary world** (i.e. get out of the house!). These sorts of activities fill your creative right brain with the images, experiences and ideas that every writer needs.

Basil Exposition

Exposition is when the storyteller gives us some factual information necessary to our understanding of the plot. Basil Exposition is the funny name of a character from the Austin Powers movies who pops up every time something needs explaining. The mentor is the most likely candidate to take on this role. A popular way of presenting exposition is during an argument or fight. People are so keen to see what happens that they hardly notice the information dump. One of my favourite ways of doing exposition is over a tasty meal in a cafe or restaurant. I call this **snaxpostion**.

BRAINSTORMING

Brainstorming is when a group of people hold a discussion to come up with ideas. I often do this in writing workshops where we are plotting out a story. We toss around different ideas, even crazy ones, before we settle on one. You can brainstorm with a friend (see the **Writer's Date**), in a writing group or even on your own. Take a sheet of paper and write down all the ideas you can think of in a story you would like to write: character names, lines of dialogue, settings, opponents, twists and turns, etc. Things you remember, even if for no apparent reason, are almost always important to you. Jot them down. Sometimes you have to work to muster interest, if someone else asks you to write about something specific. For my Roman Quests books, I wrote down all the fascinating places in the UK where you can still visit Roman ruins or see ancient artefacts. These settings helped me determine the journey my characters would take.

Breaking the Fourth Wall

On ancient Greek vases, most of the people painted there walk 'like Egyptians', just showing us their side view as they act out stories from mythology or honour the gods. But occasionally one of the drawn figures looks out at us. When a character in a movie looks straight at the camera and speaks to us, the viewer, it's called 'breaking the fourth wall', and it's a bit of a shock. (See **Kill the Dog** for an example.) In movies and TV, breaking the fourth wall is a risk; it can jolt the viewer right out of the story because there is power in the eyes. But it's easier in a book, as you can get away with addressing the reader. A famous example is the last line of *Jane Eyre* by Charlotte Brontë: 'Reader, I married him.' At the end of the first chapter of *The Time Travel Diaries* I break the fourth wall with a **cliffhanger**: 'HERE'S A TIP FOR YOU: if your headteacher sends you on a mission and warns you not to tell your parents or legal guardian about it, something is fishy.'

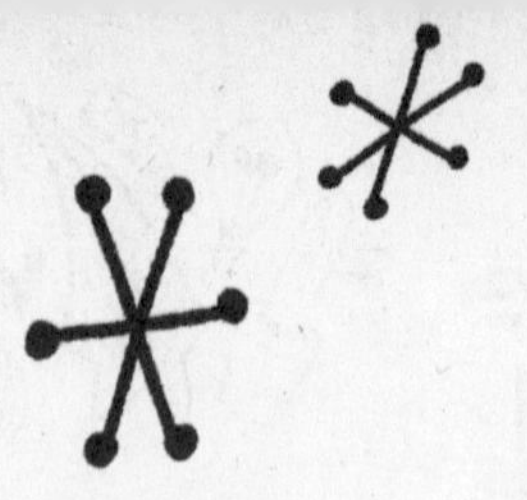

Call to Adventure

In **the hero's journey** or 'monomyth' plot template, a messenger or herald arrives near the beginning of the story and urges the hero to go an adventure. Some screenwriters call this the 'inciting incident'. The call to adventure doesn't happen in every story but it's in almost every myth-based quest. Sometimes it is the mentor who urges the hero to set out on an adventure, as in *Star Wars*, *Paddington* and *The Lord of the Rings*. Sometimes a crisis requires the hero to act, as in the *Hunger Games* and *Back to the Future*. Sometimes it's a literal call to adventure, as in *The Matrix*, when Neo gets a phone call! What happens next? Usually the **Refusal of the Call**.

Cascade of Ideas

I know I've had a good idea (see **Light Bulb Moment**) when I get a cascade of ideas. Imagine standing under a waterfall of images and words. As they splash onto your head, some get into your brain. This is the moment to write them down (see **Writer's Notebook**). Sometimes the cascade of ideas comes in the middle of the night. Once I woke at four in the morning and here are some of the phrases I jotted down in sleepy darkness:

Song stuck in head
soap bubble gas flame portal
what could you do to earn money?
Greek G'ma culture Sat
Julius Caesar in the O

They may seem like gibberish, but I know what each one means. For example, 'Song stuck in head' was my idea that my time traveller has a song from modern times stuck in their head and unconsciously hums it. Then someone from ancient times starts humming that song too! Almost all these ideas made it into my *Time Travel Diaries*.

Chapter Outline

After I've jotted down the seven beats of my overall story (which can change during the writing process), I start a chapter outline. First, I make a list numbered one to fifty (or whatever) with just a line of description for each chapter. Next, I put possible titles for chapters and a few lines about what might happen on index cards so I can shuffle them around. This is what they do in the **Writers' Room** when working on a TV series, but their cards are for each scene rather than each chapter. Then I go to my document and flesh out each chapter, using the seven beats for each one. Once you start writing, things will change and you can change the chapter outline accordingly. A chapter outline gives you a 'bird's eye view' of your story so that you can see the way it flows.

Chekhov's Gun

The Russian playwright Anton Chekhov famously said that if you have a gun somewhere on stage in the first act of a play then it must go off at some point. 'Otherwise don't put it there.' (See **Set-Ups and Payoffs**.) It doesn't have to be a gun; it could be Chekhov's Poison, Chekhov's Bomb or even Chekhov's Volcano. However, today's readers are so sophisticated that they will expect the gun, bomb or volcano to go off, so sometimes you can surprise them by making it a **red herring** that never pays off. Just having it there can be a way of giving a scene depth, because it gives you a dangerous threat constantly lingering in the background.

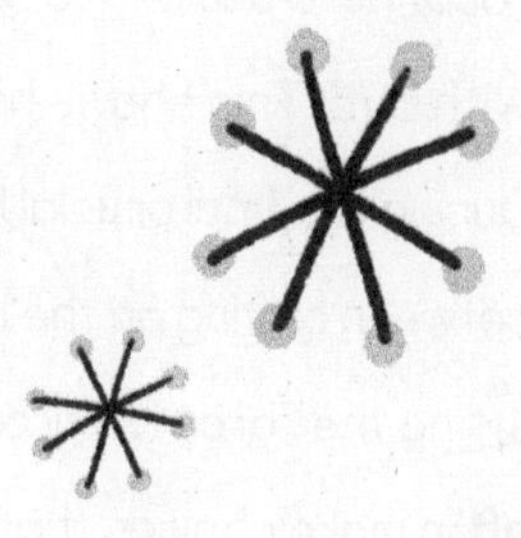

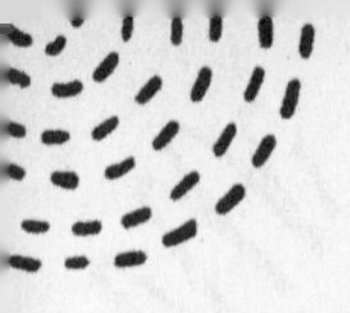

The Choice

'It is a far, far better thing that I do than I have ever done; it is a far, far better rest that I go to than I have ever known.'
Charles Dickens, last line of *A Tale of Two Cities* (1859)

At the end of a story the hero is often given a difficult choice, usually between their desire and the thing they realise they need to do. What they choose shows us if they've learned their life lesson and/or overcome their weakness. In *Despicable Me*, Gru has to choose between getting the moon, which was his original desire, and going to the girls' ballet recital. The invitation is floating next to the moon in space! In *WALL-E*, our robot hero decides to save the planet rather than hold hands with EVE. This shows he's putting aside his own desire for hers. During the final crucial battle in *Star Wars*, Luke must decide between relying on the controls in his X-wing starfighter or 'using the Force'. In great stories, the hero and the opponent often make choices that bring them closer to each other.

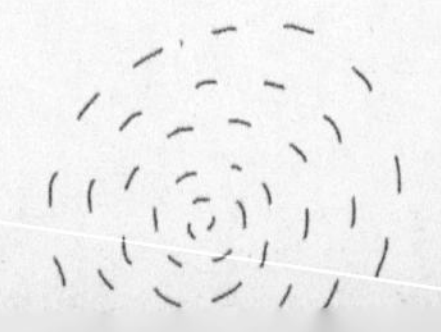

Cliché First Aid

A cliché is an expression that is popular but overused. It's lazy writing, but also an easy fix. As with **Dr Frankenstein's First Lines** or **Random Passage**, you can change a word or two to make it fresh and funny. In *The Time Travel Diaries*, my hero Alex says, in the 'cold light of a tube train' instead of the cliché 'cold light of day'. Rather than the clichéd 'cat got your tongue?', in one of my Roman Mysteries books, I used a real ancient version: 'ox tread on your tongue?' Lemons were hard to find in Roman times so instead of 'When life gives you lemons, make lemonade', I might write, 'When life gives you sour grapes, make vinegar.' Clichés can be useful however. For example, in **dialogue** clichés show that a particular character is unimaginative or lazy.

Cliffhanger

This is an oldie but a goodie. It just means ending a chapter or scene with your hero hanging from a cliff. How will they get down? Tune in next week to find out!

Of course, it doesn't have to be an actual cliff; it can be any situation where you really want to know what happens next. Suspense (which literally means 'hanging') is one of the storyteller's main tools for keeping the audience hooked. Sometimes when my character isn't in a desperate situation at the end of a scene, I might write something like, 'Little did she know what would happen next,' or similar.

TIP: When you start the next chapter, don't give the resolution immediately... make your reader wait!

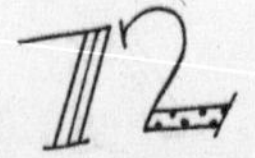

Closing Image

The popular script guru Blake Snyder said that stories are 'change machines'. He meant that your hero will learn and change as a result of the tests, trials and encounters on the journey they take. If you have an **opening image** of your hero, showing their problems and needs, and then contrast it with the closing image, you should be able to see the **arc** of how they have changed. In Pixar's *WALL-E* we start with an image of a little garbage robot all alone in a polluted world. We end with him surrounded by friends who love him in a world which, thanks to his adventure, will be made green again. Other famous closing images that show us what the character has learned can be found in *The Wizard of Oz*, *Paddington* and *Star Wars*.

Collection of Allies

An 'ally' is a helper. In many great films, the hero collects some allies to help them on their journey. Where would Dorothy be without the Scarecrow, the Tin Man and the Cowardly Lion? In *Star Wars*, R2-D2, Han Solo and Chewbacca help Luke find Princess Leia and the plans to the Death Star. In fact, it's hard to think of a story where the hero doesn't collect allies. In *The Lego Movie*, even that notorious loner Batman gets some helpers and allies. The collection of allies usually occurs just before or shortly after the hero **crosses the threshold** and enters the **World of Adventure**.

Coming up with Names

One of the questions I get asked most frequently is 'Where do you get your names?' As most of my books are set in ancient Roman times, that's easy. I get the names from ancient writings. Sometimes even from tombs and graves. Those people lived so long ago that they can't object. But for stories set in modern times you have to be careful. I thought I had come up with a clever name for the mentor in my *Time Travel Diaries*: Solomon Daisy. I even had the idea that his family name was originally Denisovich but it got changed to Daisy when Solomon's great-grandfather fled persecution in Russia. When the book was almost ready to go to print, I decided to google 'Solomon Daisy'. To my horror I discovered he was a character from a book called *Barnaby Rudge* by Charles Dickens! I have never read that book, but I must have heard the name and stored it away in my subconscious. Thankfully the works of Dickens are now out of copyright, but I should have checked earlier. Of course, if you choose a name like Oliver Brown or Sophia Smith there are bound to be thousands of others in the world with that name, which means it's safe to use.

Conflict

The word comes from the Latin to 'strike together' or clash. It's another way of referring to the **battle** (step five of the **Seven Plot Beats**). You probably love watching battles on TV or the big screen, but you don't want them in your own life. And yet you engage in conflict many times a day: when you race to get the bathroom first, when you jostle to get on the train or bus, when you disagree with someone in a discussion, when you play games and compete in sports. Without conflict (including battles, tests, trials and obstacles) the hero of a story doesn't really learn his lesson. In *The Incredibles*, it is only by battling Syndrome that Bob learns he's better using teamwork with his family. In *Despicable Me*, it is only by conflict with Vector that Gru learns the three little girls are more important than the moon. The hero in a story can lose a battle but learn something useful in the process and still end up on a higher level. In the same way, in our own lives we learn a lot about ourselves through conflict. Conflict in a story also adds suspense and keeps us turning the page to find out who wins.

Warning! Because we love our characters, we tend to make things easy for them. I sometimes put a Post-It note on my computer reminding me to add: 'MORE CONFLICT!'

Criticism

Nobody likes criticism. But remember: your editor or teacher are just trying to help you be better. They're on your side.

I have three basic reactions to criticism.

A voice in my head says:

1. *You know, I was wondering about that as I wrote it. They're definitely right.*

2. *Gosh! They might have a point. I'll try it out and see if it works.*

3. *No! I believe what I wrote there is great and I'm sticking with it.*

I end up changing some things, trying out others and leaving the rest. Trust the little voice in your head, which could be your rational left brain, and also your 'gut feeling', which is probably your intuitive right brain. Remember that in the end the story is ***yours***.

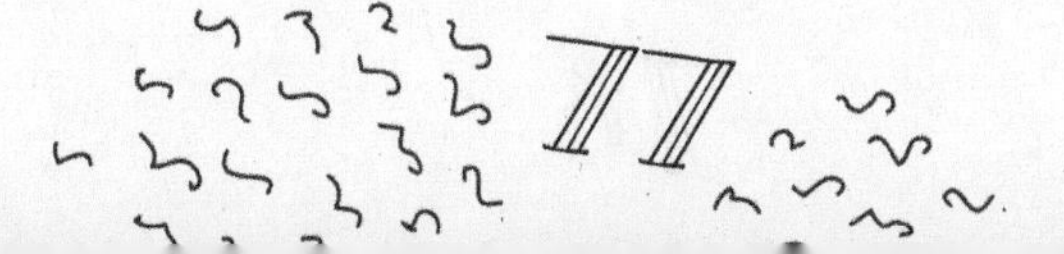

CROSSING THE THRESHOLD

'A journey of a thousand miles begins with a single step.'
Attributed to **Laozi**

That Chinese proverb reminds us that a single step can have monumental impact. In storytelling, a journey and sometimes a new act, begins with the hero stepping from his **ordinary world** into a **world of adventure**. Some screenwriters call this step ***crossing the threshold***. The word 'threshold' means the slab of stone or wooden plank at the bottom of a doorway. Every house has at least one, even if it is just a strip of metal. The threshold divides the inside from the outside, and sometimes one world from another. When Flavia Gemina steps out of her back door and into the graveyard in *The Thieves of Ostia*, she crosses a threshold. When Mattie Ross rides her pony Little Blackie through a freezing river in *True Grit*, she crosses a threshold into Indian Territory. When Katniss Everdeen steps up onto that train in the *The Hunger Games* movie, she crosses a threshold, not just because the train will take her from District 12 to the Capitol, but because the inside of the train is like being in the Capitol already. In cinema, this is often the most visually exciting moment of the whole movie.

The Cup of Cocoa

In a very exciting or dangerous story, we sometimes need to take a break from all that tension. And so does our hero. One way is to have the funny one make us laugh. Another way of giving our hero a breather is to bring them and their pals into a safe place for a while. This is like an oasis in a desert or the eye of the hurricane or the calm before the storm. Your heroes can rest and have something to eat, or at the very least a cup of cocoa. This is often where they take stock of their situation, gather their strength and form a new plan. You can have some fun at this point, and even laughter. Your heroes will need that cup of cocoa, because things are going to get intense!

The Dance

This is one of John Truby's tropes and it is one of my favourites. In a love story it's where the two lovers do something together for the first time and we see they make an amazing team. It can be a literal dance, like in *Pride and Prejudice* where Lizzy and Darcy dance for the first time and everyone else melts away. When WALL-E and EVE do their outer space ballet together the captain of the *Axiom* says, 'Define "Dancing".' Both those examples give me chills every time. It doesn't have to be a literal dance though.

Later, when the lovers are kept apart or undergoing trials, we remember that moment and root for them to get together again. It can also work for buddies. Think of Hiccup and Toothless from *How to Train Your Dragon*, when they first fly together.

Deus Ex Machina

This is Latin for 'God from a Crane'. It goes back to the days of ancient Greece and Rome, where an actor playing one of the gods would be lowered onto the stage by means of a wooden crane. In this way he seemed to come from the sky and could intervene in the story and sort out everybody's problems. Whenever a character we haven't met or an object or event we didn't know about comes out of nowhere to save the hero or change the story, that is *deus ex machina*. Two good examples come from *The Lego Movie*. When Emmet and Lucy Wildstyle are falling to certain death in a crocodile-infested river, suddenly Batman swoops down out of nowhere to save them. Near the end of the movie Emmet, who is an animated Lego figure, is taken up out of his whole world by the human who created the Lego city. Most writers try to avoid this trope because it can seem so unrealistic that it pulls you out of a story. But if it is set up properly then it can pay off brilliantly.

Dialogue

Dialogue is what people say to each other in a story. It is usually put inside inverted commas, but not always. Dialogue is reader-friendly because it breaks up big paragraphs of description and lets some white show on the page. It also brings the story alive because we can 'hear' the characters in our heads. A good tip for writing dialogue is to make the sentence length and choice of words fit each person who is speaking. A clever detective might speak in long sentences with big words. A sullen teenager might only speak in grunts and short sentences. You can have a character who speaks strangely because they are learning a language. You can even have a character who doesn't speak at all. Ideally, every bit of dialogue reveals something about the character or the story. (See also **Ninja Description**.)

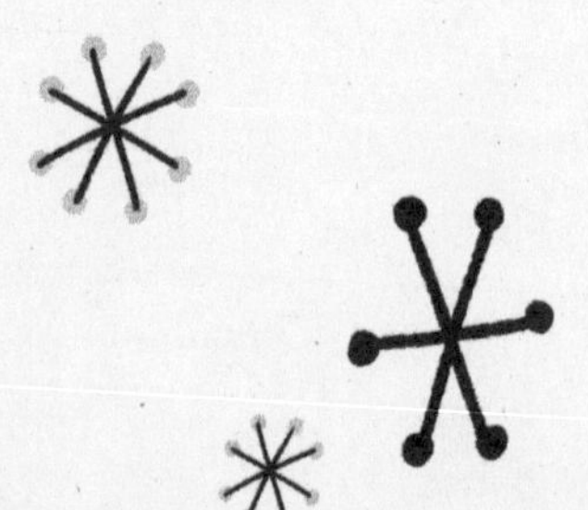

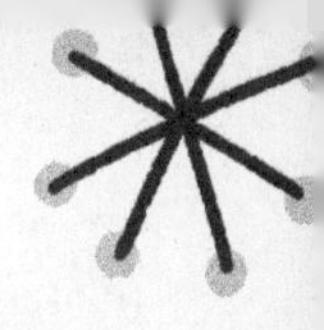

Dialogue Tags

A dialogue tag is a short phrase like 'he said' or 'she asked' that we put beside dialogue. When I had just started teaching myself to write, I jotted down as many dialogue tags as I could think of: said, asked, cried, replied, whispered, hissed, shouted, commanded, gasped, whimpered, hollered, bellowed, squeaked, purred and so forth. But then I read an essay by author Elmore Leonard who said you should only use 'he/she said' because the verb 'said' is essentially invisible. I tried using only the dialogue tag 'said' in my P.K. Pinkerton books, but my editors strongly encouraged me to put in other verbs like 'asked', 'replied' and 'cried'. One dialogue tag I do enjoy using is 'lied'. Here's an example from my *Time Travel Diaries*: 'I'm doing it for religious reasons,' I lied.

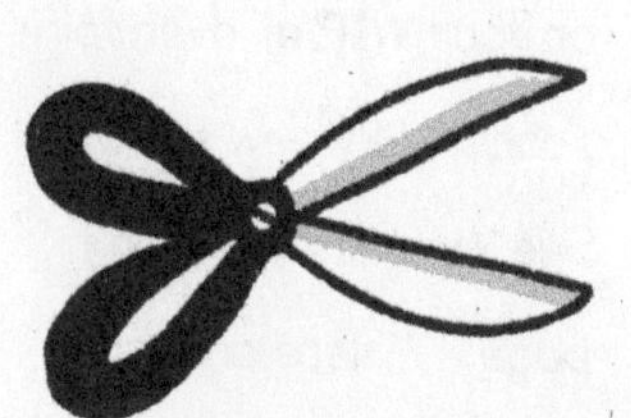

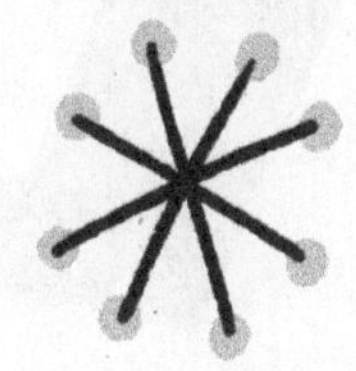

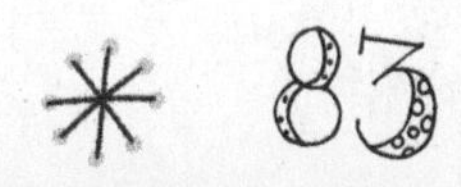

DR FRANKENSTEIN'S FIRST LINES

Stuck for an idea? Pick some of your favourite books from the shelf and write down two or three of the best first lines. Then chop them up a bit and change the names, along with one or two crucial words. You could even stitch two first lines together – or even more than two – the way Dr Frankenstein made his famous monster. This will often give you a great idea for your **WIP** or even for a completely new story. See **Workshop #3** on page 47. Here are three of my favourite first lines:

'Call me Ishmael.'

(from *Moby Dick* by Herman Melville)

'Marley was dead: to begin with.'

(from *A Christmas Carol* by Charles Dickens.)

'When Mary Lennox was sent to Misselthwaite Manor to live with her uncle everybody said she was the most disagreeable-looking child ever seen.'

(from *The Secret Garden* by Frances Hodgson Burnett)

And check out a few more books featuring some of my favourite first lines: *Stormbreaker* by Anthony Horowitz, *Charlotte's Web* by E.B. White, *Peter Pan* by J.M. Barrie and *The School of Good and Evil* by Soman Chainani.

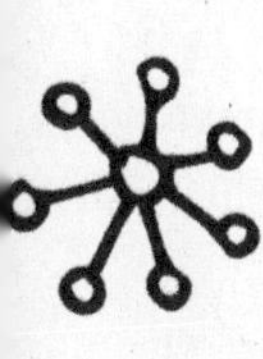
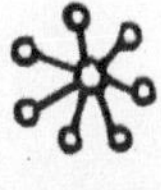
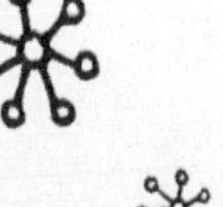

Drafts

Writing is rewriting . . . When I came to write my second book I thought, *I don't need to plan this one; I know how to plot out a story now*. Boy, was I wrong! I ended up cutting a third of it and having to write thirty-seven drafts . . . I have discovered that if you plan the book first, you don't need to do as many rewrites. But, in fact, drafts are fun. You've got down the basic story. Now you can stand back and see the whole shape of it. You can add some **set-ups** for later payoffs. Some writers first see the **theme** of their story at this point. Think of writing another draft as an opportunity to make your book even better and have fun!

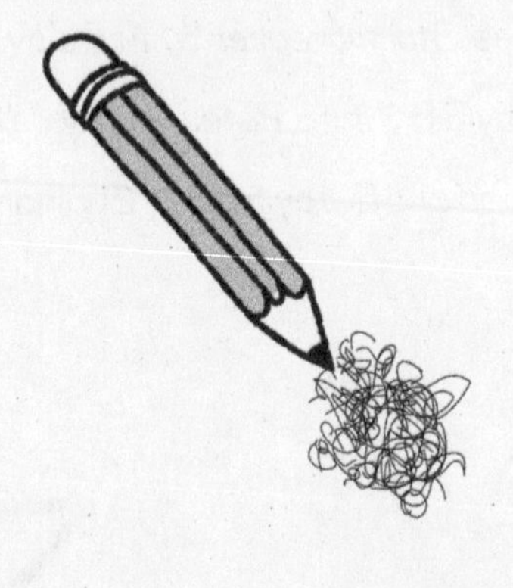

DRAT!

My friend Sophie McKenzie (author of *Girl, Missing* and many other great books) sometimes teaches creative writing to adults. One of her favourite tips is to include a D.R.A.T. (Desperate Race Against Time). When your hero has to achieve their goal in a limited time it adds suspense, especially if the **stakes** are high. Some authors call this the 'ticking clock' and in many thrillers this is a literal ticking clock, where a bomb must be defused before it goes *kablooey!* This trope is used in almost every *James Bond* and *Mission Impossible* movie. In other stories a hostage must be rescued or the antidote must reach the victim by a deadline or they will be . . . dead. In the movie *Coco* we are reminded of DRAT as we see Miguel turning slowly into a skeleton. Marty McFly is starting to disappear from his photos and must go *Back to the Future* at the exact moment lightning strikes the clock tower. In *Mary Poppins Returns*, they have to get a document to the bank before Big Ben chimes midnight. DRAT! It's a Desperate Race Against Time!

Draw Your Characters

One of the ways I get ideas for characters is to use faces of people I don't know, especially musicians. When I was writing my Roman Mysteries I used songs by a California smooth-jazz guitarist called Larry Carlton to imagine some of my settings. It was the olden days when there were still music CDs with covers, so I made a drawing of Larry Carlton, added a beard and got Doctor Mordecai, who is Jonathan's father and a kind of mentor. I used a photo of an Italian girl I met in Ostia to draw Flavia and copied a boy from an ancient Roman painting to be Jonathan. You might not think drawing your characters is proper writing . . . but it is! It's writing with your right brain. Your drawings don't have to be brilliant or even good. Just **have fun!**

Elevator Pitch

The definition of the verb to pitch is 'to throw roughly or casually'. In the world of storytelling, the thing you toss out is the idea for your book, movie or platform game. Imagine that one day you find yourself in an elevator (the American word for a 'lift') and you recognise a man in a baseball cap. Without thinking you cry, 'You're Steven Spielberg! I'm your biggest fan. I love *Jaws*, *Raiders of the Lost Ark* and *Jurassic Park*. I hope to write movies one day.' He grins at you and punches the button for the penthouse. 'I'm always looking for good stories,' he says. 'What have you got for me?' You now have five floors to pitch him your idea for a movie. But that doesn't give you long, so you've got to do it in just a few sentences. Thankfully you learned it by heart, ready for just such an opportunity. Ready, steady . . . pitch!

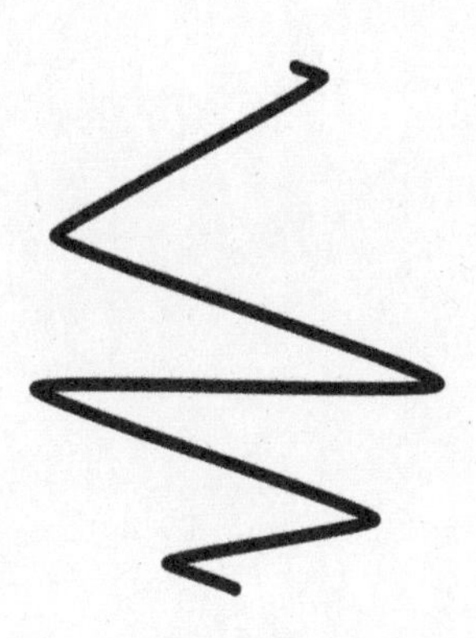

Empathy Machines

A famous American film critic named Roger Ebert called movies 'the most powerful empathy machines in all the arts', but I'm not sure I agree. I adore movies, but I wonder if books are not even more powerful. You don't just sit passively and watch as with cinema, but you actively participate as your imagination works with the writer's words to create a world in your head. A book can tell you more clearly what a character is feeling and what motivates them. If a movie can put you in someone else's shoes, then a book can put you in someone else's head! This is a truly extraordinary thing.

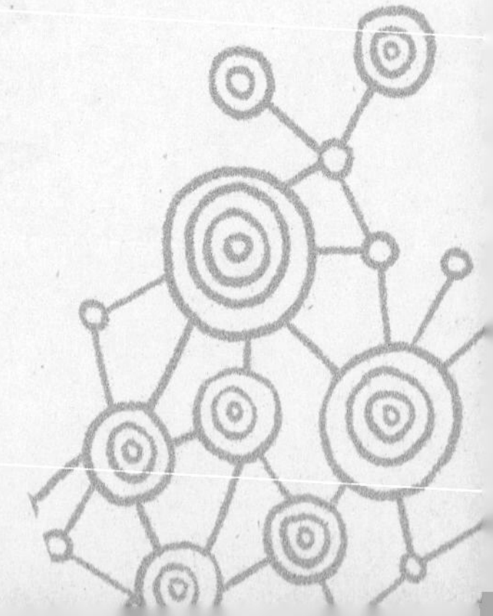

Fan Fiction

When someone reads, watches or hears a story and loves the character, they sometimes want more. So they create a new story using the same characters. This is not a recent practice but goes right back to ancient times. The Latin poet Virgil wrote his epic masterpiece *The Aeneid* based on characters and plot structure taken from Homer's two oral poems, the *Iliad* and the *Odyssey*. One of my favourite childhood books, *The Once and Future King* by T. H. White, was a riff on a book called *Le Morte d'Arthur*, written in 1485. (See also **Magpie!**) Writing fan fiction is a great way to get started as a writer and find your voice, but if you are thinking of publishing it, BE CAREFUL! You don't want to be sued for plagiarism, which is when you steal great blocks of someone else's writing or even their ideas.

FINDING YOUR VOICE

People often talk about the 'voice' of an author. That is just another way of saying their style of writing. Surprisingly, a good way to find your unique voice is by imitation. **Magpie** ideas, phrases and characters you like. Or you can try writing **fan fiction**. Choose an author you love and try writing in their style. The reason you love that person's writing is probably because it chimes with something deep inside you. It's the way you would like to write. Let them teach you. Look at some of their first lines. Analyse the first paragraph of your favourite book by that author. Is it written in present tense or past tense? First person? Third person? How long are the sentences? Does the author use simple words or long ones? Write a paragraph copying that author's style, but with a different hero and setting. In the past, this is how artists learned to paint: by copying the old masters. When Goosebumps author R. L. Stine was just starting out as a writer he spent a whole summer writing a book in the style of an author he admired. Like him, if you start by imitating other authors' styles, you will soon find your own voice.

Fish Out of Water

The expression 'fish out of water' is used for someone out of their element. When your main character crosses the threshold into the **world of adventure**, they are often totally clueless. This can be very dramatic or funny, or both. A funny example of a 'fish out of water' in movies is when Paddington first goes into the Browns' bathroom. He doesn't know how this world 'works'. Dorothy is a fish out of water when she reaches Oz, as is WALL-E when he arrives on the *Axiom* spaceship. Alice is definitely a fish out of water in Wonderland! There are lots of dramatic examples from *Finding Nemo*, including a few scenes when Nemo is literally a 'fish out of water'.

GeNre

This word comes from the Latin 'genus' and means 'a type of thing'. It's a fancy word for the type of story you're writing or film you're making. Examples of different genres are Mystery, Horror, Fantasy, Romance, Science Fiction, Historical and Adventure. You can mix genres as I do in my Roman Mysteries, which some call History-Mystery, and in my time-travel books, which are a blend of Science Fiction and Historical. You can have sub-genres and even no genre. You can even make up a totally new genre. It's just another box to help you figure out what your story is, or isn't, about.

Get It Down!

If inspiration strikes and you have an idea for a scene, Get It Down! Don't worry if the scene occurs somewhere in the middle of your story or even if you haven't written the story to go with it. Do a stream of consciousness **vomit draft** like you do your **morning pages**. Keep your hand moving. Even when you think you've finished, force your hand to keep writing and your right brain to keep coming up with images and ideas. Later you can go back and let your left brain edit it. Interestingly, many authors say that when they look back over their work, they can't actually tell the difference between the passages written under the flow of inspiration and passages ground out through clenched determination. But don't let that discourage you from getting it down if inspiration strikes . . . even in the middle of the night. Incidentally, that is how some of the most famous pop songs were written: in the middle of the night. (See **The Muse**.)

Have Fun!

I have a Post-It note on my computer with a grinning cartoon sun and the words 'Have Fun!' Your creative right brain likes to play. It doesn't like homework. Whenever writing feels like a burden and not a joy, STOP! Take a few minutes to play. Write a haiku. Sketch a scene with cartoon or stick figures. Or just write a silly 'vomit paragraph' (see **Vomit Draft**). Say to yourself, 'This paragraph doesn't matter . . . I'm just having fun.' Once the pressure is off, your imagination will soar. I recently had a revelation: the very act of typing or moving a pen across paper will bring new ideas. That may be one reason we find it so hard to ACTUALLY START WRITING every morning. Our control-freak left brain knows that the imaginative right brain is going to be taking part. And when the imagination is involved, anything can happen in our stories.

HELP!

'Help!' you wail. 'Every time I sit down to write, something comes to distract me . . .' In this case, do the **Morning Pages**. By doing them you will be getting rid of all the negative energy in your head and you will also be training yourself to write daily.

'Help!' you moan. 'I can't write! I've tried and I'm rubbish. I'll never be any good.' Start doing **Morning Pages** every day. And remember that only you can tell stories about your life and the things important to you.

'Help!' you cry. 'I'm stuck! I have to write something and I'm in a panic! I have no idea what to write about!' In this case, try **Random Passage** or **Dr Frankenstein's First Lines**. Try **Walking Solves Problems**. And if you still can't think of anything just do a **vomit draft** of a story about someone who has to write and can't think what to write! Remember: a good way to start a story is: Blank had a problem . . .

Heritage Characters

When you have a long-running series of books, films or platform games, some of the characters are bound to grow older. They can then appear in sequels as the mentor. The expression 'heritage characters' first hit my radar when *Star Wars: The Force Awakens* came out in 2015, nearly forty years after *Star Wars*. Luke, Leia and Han Solo all appear, but are much older. I used this idea for my Roman Quests series, a spin-off of my Roman Mysteries. Flavia, Nubia, Jonathan and Lupus are now in their mid-twenties and appear mainly to support the real main characters, Juba and his brother Fronto and sister Ursula. In real life, that's what happens to many of us as we get older: although we will always be the hero of our own life, we begin to take on the role of advisor and helper to others. I hope I can be a bit of a mentor to YOU in your quest to become a storyteller. I guess that would make this book the talisman!

The Hero's Journey

In 1949 an anthropologist named Joseph Campbell published a book called *The Hero with a Thousand Faces*. He claimed that all cultures in the past as well as the present have some kind of myth where a hero goes on a quest, undergoes tests and trials and returns home ready to be a leader. Campbell pointed out more than a dozen steps these mythic stories all have in common. The book became popular in the mid-1970s and a few Hollywood screenwriters wondered if the so-called hero's journey would work as plot structure. The first director to try it out was George Lucas and the film was *Star Wars*. If you google 'The Hero's Journey' or 'monomyth', you will see the dozen or so steps. They include the **Call to Adventure**, the **Refusal of the Call** and the **Mentor**. One of the most powerful steps is the **Visit to Death**.

The Inner Journey

Some screenwriters, like Christopher Vogler and Michael Hague, talk about an inner journey in addition to the outer hero's journey. The inner journey is when the hero learns what they need to know to live a better life. The outer journey is simply to get the desire. You could also call the inner journey the 'spiritual journey'. As the hero is going on the quest, undergoing trials and tests and battles, they are learning how to realise their potential.

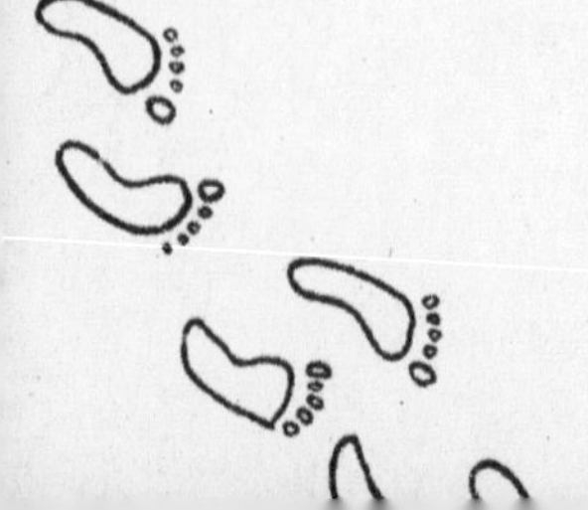

Kill the Dog

Hollywood screenwriter Blake Snyder 'invented' the phrase '**save the cat**' to show that a character is a nice guy or gal. Some storytellers do a twist on this and have the main character act badly to show that they're NOT nice. I first noticed this watching the Netflix series for adults *House of Cards*. In the very first scene of the very first episode, a man comes out of his house to find a dog has been hit by a car. The dog is still alive and in pain. 'It's the Whartons' dog,' says our 'hero' Frank Underwood. 'It's not gonna make it.' As he begins to strangle the dog he looks out at us the viewer and says, 'Moments like this require someone who will do the unpleasant thing, the necessary thing . . . No more pain.' His action is humane, but also kind of horrible. That scene tells us everything we need to know about his character.

Left Brain

In this book I criticise the left brain a lot, but in fact I LOVE my left brain! Yes, it is bossy, but it is also a wordsmith. Yes, it is rigid, but it knows cool formulas and structures that work. Yes, it is critical, but sometimes we need a critical editor to get our **vomit draft** looking like a real story. If Right Brain is colour, Left Brain is black and white. Right Brain is fuzzy and has no borders. Left Brain stays inside the lines. Yes, it's simplistic but the whole concept of two sides of the brain is very Left Brain. Where would I be without my left brain? I'd be in a swamp of mad colours, sounds, sights and smells saying, 'Groovy! . . . Cool! . . . Awesome!' and never getting any work done.

- VERBAL
- BOSSY
- CLEVER
- OBSESSIVE
- RATIONAL
- CRITICAL

Life Lesson

'Know thyself.'
Ancient Greek slogan from the
Temple of Apollo at Delphi

Some people like to call the moral of a story the 'life lesson'. I call it the 'knowledge'. Truby calls it the 'self-revelation'. You could even call it the 'light bulb moment'. Whatever you call it, we need it desperately. Not just on our journeys and in the big battles in our lives, but every day. We need to learn how to live our best life, and stories help us do that. For me, this is why John Truby's seven-step structure is the most valuable; because he highlights that moment of revelation. Ancient Greek philosophers and modern prophets encourage us to know ourselves. As we read stories but especially as we write, we learn about how to overcome our weaknesses and make them our strengths.

Light Bulb Moment

In some old cartoons (and *The Lego Movie*) you know when a character has just had a good idea because a light bulb suddenly appears over their head and lights up with a *ding!* That's actually what it feels like sometimes when you have a good idea. I often get the light bulb moment when I am telling someone about my story. It's not that they have said anything, but rather that saying things out loud helps me clarify my thinking. It's almost as if the two sides of my brain are having a conversation. The left brain is blathering on and suddenly the right brain goes *DING!*

Love the Underdog

One way to get the reader or audience to immediately warm to your hero is to have them bullied by those who are bigger and more powerful at the beginning of a story. We all know what that feels like, and we empathise. If the hero endures the bullying with humour and fortitude we love them even more. A famous example is Harry Potter, who is forced by the beastly Dursley family to sleep under the stairs. I use the underdog idea

at the beginning of *The Time Travel Diaries*, where kids at Alex's school call him 'Wimpy' and the new boy mugs him for his crisps.

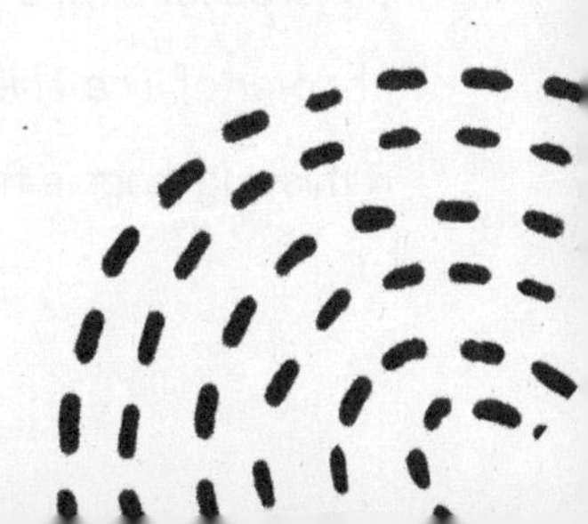

Magpie

Magpies are notorious thieves. Like a magpie going from place to place to find bright shiny things, you can also get your ideas from different sources. The Latin poet Virgil borrowed ideas from the Greek poet Homer. Shakespeare lifted storylines from Plutarch, a Greek author who lived more than 1400 years earlier.

Copying from one source is plagiarism. But it's OK to gather ideas and short lines from lots of different places so long as you change key elements and words to make them yours.

In my second Roman Mystery I got the idea for the first line from a Nancy Drew novel where someone screams 'Nancy! Look out!' It turns out she's only about to slop a tray of hot chocolate (see **First Lines**). In my fourth Roman Mystery, *The Assassins of Rome*, I got the idea for the opening scene from a comic strip panel about a fat orange cat named Garfield! And in the first chapter of *The Thieves of Ostia*, I magpied the idea of a thieving magpie from *Postman Pat*!

Maguffin

Sometimes also spelled 'MacGuffin', this is an invented word used by screenwriters to stand for something the hero wants. Unlike a proper desire, the Maguffin has no importance in itself; it's just a device to get the hero to go on a quest. In fact, the hero often forgets about it by the end of the story. Some good examples are the plans to the Death Star in *Star Wars*, the diamond necklace in *Titanic* and the 'Piece of Resistance' in *The Lego Movie*. The famous movie director Alfred Hitchcock popularised this term when he remarked that the Maguffin is the thing that the spies are after, although the people watching the movie don't really care about it.

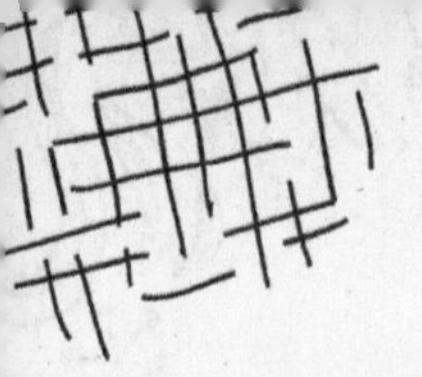

In Medias Res

This is Latin for 'In the Middle of Things'. It's often a good idea to start your story at a moment of tension or excitement. In my first P. K. Pinkerton book I start with my hero down a mineshaft with the opponent closing in. This exciting first chapter acts as a kind of prologue. You can then use the next chapter to start the story, but hopefully the reader is hooked. This is what some writers call a **running start**.

yes

Midpoint

There is often magic in the middle of a story. Try opening a book right at the middle and I'll bet something very important happens there. The hero thinks they have achieved their desire. Maybe they get to kiss someone. Or get a reward. Sometimes it's their lowest moment. Sometimes a high point is quickly followed by a low point. Or vice versa. But we're only halfway through the story! It's just a false victory or defeat. The hero still has the **battle** to come and before that they'll need to undergo tests and training. In many stories with a **three-act structure**, the second act is almost twice as long as the first and third acts, so this midpoint is useful because it breaks that long middle act into two parts. Some writers call this the **point of no return**, but I like to think of that as the moment our main character first **crosses the threshold** into the **world of adventure**.

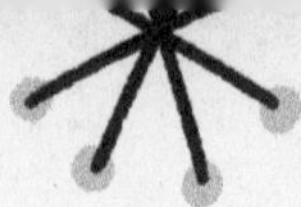

The Miniature

Remember the doll's house version of the Browns' house in *Paddington*? The pop-up book of London in *Paddington 2*? Doc Brown's working models of how to get back to the present in the *Back to the Future* trilogy? The cowboys and Romans in all three *Night in the Museum* movies? The hologram of Princess Leia in *Star Wars*? All these are miniatures. They often illustrate a plot beat or remind us where we are in the story. In the first Paddington movie, the model train in Mr Gruber's shop tells us his story in a few memorable moments and the dolls' house in the attic shows us how the Browns are doing. The miniature has an almost magical appeal. Because of its visual impact, it is usually most effective in films, but books can have it too. *Alice in Wonderland* is one famous example. Some writers have based entire stories around miniature worlds: *Stuart Little, The Borrowers* and *Honey, I Shrunk the Kids*.

THE MONTAGE

When the hero goes to the **world of adventure** they might need to learn a new skill or instrument. This can take a long time and can be quite boring. In a book and especially a movie, the hero often has to train for the battle. Filmmakers like to show the hero's progress over a long time with lots of very short scenes or images, often put to upbeat music. This is called a 'montage' and it shows the hero's progress in just a few minutes. The most common is the 'Training Montage'. You will also spot the 'Having Fun Montage', a 'Getting Used to the New World Montage' and lots more. I tried to do a 'Travelling Montage' in my book *Return to Rome* by writing just one sentence for each place my characters passed through. It's easier when you can have music. In *Despicable Me* we see Gru being mean, to the tune of 'I'm Having a Bad, Bad Day'. In *Despicable Me 2* we see him being happy to 'Happy'. And in the classic example of a 'training montage', Rocky – the would-be boxer – runs, punches and sweats to the tune 'Gonna Fly Now' which became the theme song of all the *Rocky* movies.

MORNING PAGES

This is a brilliant writer's tool I got from Julia Cameron, who wrote a book called *The Artist's Way*, about how to release your creativity. She suggests doing the Morning Pages when you are blocked or can't think what to write. As soon as you get up, before brushing your teeth or eating breakfast or anything (except using the toilet), you should get out three sheets of lined paper and write. Don't edit, don't worry about messiness or spelling – the only rule is to keep your hand moving. You start by writing down your fears, worries and frustrations. You write until you have filled all three sheets and only then do you stop. Although you are using words, this is very much a right brain activity, and be warned: your critical left brain won't like it. If you can't think what to write, just write 'I can't think what to write' until you have filled all three sheets. It will take you about ten to twenty minutes. Afterwards you can shred what you've written so nobody will ever see it. Do the same thing the next day, and the next. After a few weeks, days or even minutes of doing this you find you are writing something you didn't plan. Once you have got rid of all the fears and worries that bung up your subconscious, your creativity can begin to flow! At this point you might want to stop shredding your sheets because you now have the idea for a story.

The Muse

The ancient Greeks and Romans believed that when you wrote poetry you needed a divine spirit called the Muse to help you.

Homer started his epic poem *The Odyssey* with the words: 'Tell me, O Muse, about the man . . .' and in *The Iliad* he begins: 'Sing about the anger, O Goddess . . .' Even today writers sometimes have an almost spiritual experience when ideas seem to come from outside themself or from very deep within. It doesn't happen often, but when it does it is very exciting. Once or twice I have been writing and the characters start to act of their own accord, not sticking to my plot outline. I go with it, but just because it seemed to come from somewhere else doesn't always mean it's right for the story. You have to come back later with your analytical left brain and see if it works. Sometimes an idea for character or story comes fully formed when you're not even writing. Whether it is a strange alchemy of right and left brain working together, or real divine inspiration, I don't know. All I know is that you must not ignore it, but get it down!

Ninja Description

When you write a story you must paint a picture of your characters and setting, but readers tend to skip over big blocks of description, so how to do this? Best just use a few lines of description and scatter the rest in secretly. One of my best tips is to use short descriptive sentences instead of **dialogue tags** ('he said', 'she asked', etc.). By putting a little action,

colour and movement next to the dialogue, not only will it tell us who's speaking but it is a sneaky way to make an image in your reader's right brain and help the story come alive. Here's an example of how you can give the same bit of dialogue a completely different feeling with ninja description.

'I'm too young,' he said.

This is the plain version. It's fine. Now we're going to slip in some description without you being aware of it, like a ninja.

He shook his head. 'I'm too young.'

With this you might get a brief flicker of movement as you read 'shook his head'.

He laughed. 'I'm too young.'

With this one you might 'see' someone's head going back and 'hear' the laugh.

He hung his head. 'I'm too young.'

Not only do you 'see' his head go down, but you feel his disappointment.

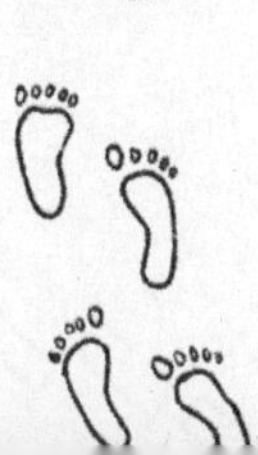

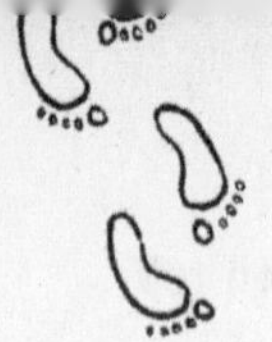

He shrugged. 'I'm too young.'

He doesn't really care . . . or does he? But we can 'see' it happening.

His handsome face went as white
as a marshmallow. 'I'm too young.'

This one has some added drama. (And I tried to use **cliché first aid.**)

His yellow plastic chair fell back with a clatter
as he jumped up. 'I'm too young.'

We've added colour, movement, sound and drama.

A friend of mine remarked that these phrases are a bit like stage directions in a play only with added colour, smell and emotions. Look for examples of ninja description in your favourite authors and see how the best writers do it.

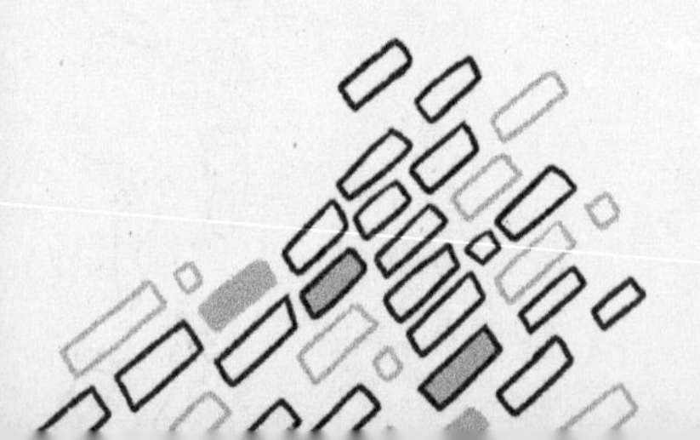

Novel versus Screenplay

Lots of people tell me they want to write a screenplay. But I advise them to write a novel using screenplay structure and tropes (like the ones in this book). That way you will always have the book. Once you sell a screenplay it's no longer yours – the new owners can do whatever they like with it. They can set your story in space instead of ancient Rome. They can make the hero a boy rather than a girl, or vice versa. They can decide not to make it into a film at all, but just leave it gathering dust on a shelf somewhere. Someone once saw a famous author at a party. 'I just saw the movie based on your novel,' he said. 'It's a shame what they've done to your book.' 'They haven't done anything to my book,' replied the author. 'It's right up there on the shelf.'

The Nubia

> *'"What is Muntulumpus?" asked Nubia.'*
> Caroline Lawrence, *The Secrets of Vesuvius*

This is a character who – like the audience – is new to the world and doesn't always understand how things work. So they can ask about the things we don't understand either. In my Roman Mysteries, Nubia the slave girl is the audience surrogate as Flavia teaches her about daily life in ancient Rome. This character can also be useful for exposition, but unlike **Basil Exposition**, they know nothing. Some writers call this character the 'Watson', after Doctor Watson in Sherlock Holmes. When Sherlock Holmes explains things to Watson, the author is really explaining them to the reader without making us feel stupid.

on the Nose

Screenwriters often refer to a bit of action or dialogue as 'on the nose' when they mean it's so obvious as to be unbelievable. People rarely say exactly what they feel and think in real life, but they show it in many ways.

Here's an example of on-the-nose dialogue: 'Are you upset that everybody in class was teasing you?' asked Abby. 'Yes.' Abe hung his head. 'It really hurt my feelings and now I'm going home to have a good cry.'

Here's a less on-the-nose way he might respond. 'I couldn't care less!' Abe clenched his fists. 'They're all idiots!' In the second example Abe's not saying what he feels, but we still know he's been hurt.

You can avoid lots of on-the-nose blunders by applying the principle **Show Don't Tell**.

OPENING IMAGE

'When Mary Lennox was sent to Misselthwaite Manor to live with her uncle, everybody said she was the most disagreeable-looking child ever seen.'
Frances Hodgson Burnett, *The Secret Garden*

Some stories start with a powerful opening image that shows the hero 'before' their transformation. This can then be bookended with an image that shows them 'after': the **closing image**. Next time you watch a movie, before you get caught up in the story, remember the opening image. Then at the end try to call that image to mind. When bookending occurs it can be a thing of beauty. This concept also works in books, with the **first lines** and the final lines. Try it with *Huckleberry Finn*, *The Secret Garden* and *Charlotte's Web*. Book series also do this.

In my Roman Mysteries series, the first word of *The Thieves of Ostia* is 'Flavia', the name of my hero, and the last word of *The Man from Pomegranate Street*, the final book in the series, is the name of the man she marries.

The Opponent

Your hero will have many opponents in their story, but it's often good to have one main opponent. Sometimes the opponent is

truly evil, like Sauron from *The Lord of the Rings* or a James Bond supervillain. Or they are only partly

evil, like Syndrome from *The Incredibles*. Or maybe even funny evil, like Dr Evil from *Austin Powers*. But the opponent does not have to be evil at all. They are just someone who clashes with your hero as they go for their desire. The opponent can even be a friend or family member. In a romance story, the opponent is often the boyfriend or girlfriend. In my favourite films, the hero and the opponent learn from each other and end up being friends, or at least not enemies any more. I recently had a revelation. In the best stories, the hero learns that the opponent is human with their own story and a valid point of view, and that maybe they are even more important than the object of desire. Sometimes the opponent is an obstacle or an inanimate object, like a volcano in my book *The Secrets of Vesuvius*. In a mystery the opponent is hidden.

Ordinary World

The hero's ordinary world may be ordinary to them, but it's utterly fascinating to us. Have you ever gone on holiday to another place and when you got back your home seemed strange and fresh for a while? That's what we as writers have to do: to look at our own world and lives with fresh eyes, trying to see it as others do. You might think your world is dull and boring, but I can assure you: it's not. You live in a unique place and time. Write about it! Then take your hero out of that world into a **world of adventure**. Then bring them back to their ordinary world and see how their adventure has changed them. That's what I did in *The Time Travel Diaries*. When Alex returns from the past to his own time, he sees it with new eyes.

Origin Story

An origin story introduces the hero and their world. In fantasy and sci-fi stories the hero often discovers their special power or calling in the first instalment. In *Star Wars*, Luke Skywalker discovers he has 'the Force'. In *The Matrix*, Neo discovers he is 'the One'. In *The Thieves of Ostia*, Flavia discovers she is a good dectective. Often the hero is an apparent misfit who has just not found his or her own place in the world. Origin stories encourage us to think about our own life stories. People can now attend seminars to write (or rewrite) an origin story for themselves or their business.

Panic

All these fun formulas for plot, characters and page-turnability make it sound easy. But sometimes a story just doesn't come together and . . . I panic! Perhaps I didn't plot it out well enough to begin with or my **theme** isn't strong enough. But stories are organic – they grow – and it may be that my story has grown into something else. Maybe I have a deadline for the first draft and it's not done. Panic!

Whenever I'm panicking I go for a walk (see **Walking Solves Problems**) and I talk about it out loud to myself (see **Talk About It**). At least these days people don't think you're crazy when you talk to yourself; if you have earbuds they'll just assume you're on the phone. Sometimes I record myself talking. When I come back from my walk I make notes on what I said. Or I do continuous writing (as with the **Morning Pages**). You've got to step back from your story sometimes and see it as a jewel in your hand. As you turn it this way and that, you can see the different facets and the overall colour.

Pixar

Pixar is the Shakespeare of our times. If you want to learn how to write powerful, life-changing stories, study the masterpieces produced by the writers at the Pixar studios: *Finding Nemo*, the Toy Story films, *WALL-E* and *Up*, just to name a few. A free pdf called Pixar's 22 *Rules of Storytelling*, is easy to find online; I often glance at it. You can even do a free online course called 'The Art of Storytelling', taught by Pixar writers at the Khan Academy. I highly recommend it.

Plot Coupons

Plot coupons is where the hero and his friends have to get different things or pass certain tests before they can get the ultimate object of desire. This 'collect-the-coupons' trope often occurs in quest stories where the objects are supernaturally linked to the desired goal. In my sixth Roman Mystery, *The Twelve Tasks of Flavia Gemina*, the demi-god Hercules appears to Flavia in a dream and urges her to complete twelve tasks (like Hercules!), promising that the answer to a mystery will then be supplied to her. The expression 'Plot Coupons' was invented in 1986 by a brilliant Classics professor and fan of sci-fi called Nick Lowe. Like the creators of the term **Rubber Ducky**, he wrote it scornfully, but it is actually quite helpful.

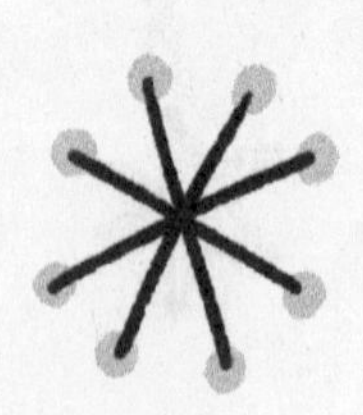

THE POINT OF NO RETURN

This is the point in the story when the hero is committed to their adventure. In my first book, *The Thieves of Ostia*, Flavia goes into the graveyard and the back door slams behind her. There is no doorknob on the outside, so for her there is no going back. She is now committed to following the magpie through the woods to find his nest. This is her point of no return. I have noticed that this step often occurs at the moment the hero crosses the threshold into the world of adventure at the beginning of Act Two in a **three-act structure**. Of course, Flavia does eventually get back, but in a surprising way and only after escaping some **opponents** with the help of a new friend.

POV

POV (or P.O.V.) is a term writers and moviemakers use to stand for 'Point of View'. Not just first person or third person, but whose point of view the whole story is told from. In my Roman Mysteries I unfold the stories from the POV of Flavia and her three friends. It's as if we are watching over their shoulder, with occasional glimpses into their thoughts and feelings. If you don't have an idea for a story you can always retell a famous fairy tale from the opponent's POV (*Wicked*) or use minor characters from a Shakespeare play (*Rosencrantz and Guildenstern are Dead*).

Primal

This is something I learned from script guru Blake Snyder's books about screenwriting. A story is primal if it involves our most basic human needs: getting food, finding shelter, finding love, raising children, protecting our family and above all: survival. Blake mischievously invented an imaginary caveman

OH NO

named Og to whom he pitches his story. Would Og care about finding the plans to the Death Star in *Star Wars*?

Yes, but only if his family and way of life was threatened. Og would understand WALL-E's loneliness, his love for EVE and his desire to save the planet. But most of all, Og would appreciate stories like *Jurassic World* or *Jaws*, where something big and scary is trying to eat you!

Primary Sources

People often ask me where I get my ideas. One answer is from primary sources. A primary source is just a fancy way of saying something written in the original time period. A 'secondary source' would be what someone else wrote afterwards in order to interpret it. E.g. the Bible is a primary source and all the commentaries and retellings are secondary sources. Because I write books with ancient historical settings, primary sources are usually written in Latin, Greek or Hebrew. I got the idea for one of my opponents from a two-line Latin epigram by the Roman poet Martial. The short poem is about a handsome dwarf. 'If you saw just his head while he was sitting, you'd think he was the hero Hector. But if you saw him standing up, you'd think he was Hector's little boy.' Much of my book about the eruption of Vesuvius is based on two letters by Pliny the Younger, who was sixteen when the event occurred. He was an eyewitness himself but also took notes from other eyewitnesses. Reading the primary sources, whether in their original language or in translation, gets you inside the heads of people who lived in other times and places.

Put It in the Freezer

In an episode of the TV series *Friends*, a character called Joey starts reading a book so scary that he puts it in the freezer. (It's *The Shining*, a horror story by bestselling author Stephen King.) I have a slightly different reason to put a book in the freezer. When you have finished a story or book and aren't sure what to do next, put it in the freezer to let it 'cool off' and start to work on something else (see ***WIP***). In other words, don't look at it for a few weeks or more if possible. That way, when you pick it up again, you will be looking at it with fresh eyes.

P.S. Obviously you don't have to literally keep it in the freezer, but in a drawer or perhaps a virtual folder called 'Freezer'.

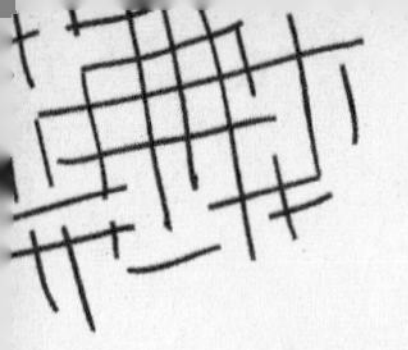

Random Passage

'I declare after all there is no enjoyment like reading!'
Jane Austen (on the £10 note)

Can't think what to write about? Stuck in the middle of your story? Feeling bored and frustrated with writing? Go into a room with lots of books: your bedroom, a library, even a bookstore. Pick one off the shelf. Open it. Start reading. If you don't like it, choose another until you find a passage that grabs you. You might see things the writer does that you like. You might see things you don't like. You admire the simplicity. Or the complexity. Or you hate them. Often you will find that after reading just a few pages you feel inspired again. This is a great way of filling up your refrigerator of ideas when you feel empty. I don't know why it works so well, but it does. If you really like the passage you're reading, try rewriting it with your characters and your setting. (See ***Finding Your Voice*** and ***Magpie***.)

READ OUT LOUD

A crucial step in polishing your story is to read it out loud at least once. You don't have to do this in front of an audience or even one other person, although you might want to do that later. First of all, just close your door and read it out loud to yourself. Sometimes people say of a certain actor, 'I could listen to him read the phone book,' meaning that actor can make even the dullest text exciting just by the way they use their voice. DON'T read your book like that! Instead, read it in a monotone, without intonation, so that the words you've written have to do all the work. Reading out loud forces you to slow down. It helps you hear things that don't work, especially repetition of words and phrases. I'll never forget the time I attended an event by a respected author who introduced her reading with the apology, 'This passage is a little bit garbled . . .' My first thought was, *Then why choose this passage to read?* My second thought was, *If you'd read it out loud when you were polishing it, then you could have fixed it!*

Red Herring

A 'red herring' is a clue that leads nowhere or sometimes even points in the wrong direction. Possibly named after a kipper, a type of fish so smelly that it confuses the noses of tracking dogs, it is a favourite trick used by crime and mystery writers. J. K. Rowling, an author who loves planning her books, once confessed on Twitter that in her vast, colour-coded outlines she sometimes uses red ink for red herrings. In *Zootropolis*, bunny detective Judy Hopps is warned of Night Howlers. She thinks that refers to wolves, until near the end when she finds out what it really refers to. In *Wonder Woman* we are led to believe that General Ludendorff is the war god Ares in disguise, but this is a red herring; Ares is somebody else entirely.

Red Shirt

In the 1960s sci-fi TV show *Star Trek* the crew of the Starship Enterprise wore three different-coloured shirts: command crew wore mustard yellow, science officers wore blue and engineering crew wore red. Whenever Captain Kirk beamed down to a new planet he would take a science officer or two (usually Mr Spock and/or Dr McCoy) and a miscellaneous crew member in a red shirt, someone we had never met before. That anonymous 'Red Shirt' almost always died, to show that the **stakes** were high: life or death! This became such a common occurrence that the term 'Red Shirt' is now used for any stock character who will probably die before we get to know them. Examples include *Jurassic World*, when some brave troopers get gobbled by a giant dinosaur, and *Monty Python and the Holy Grail*, where three anonymous knights are sent to fight the Killer Rabbit . . . and die.

Refusal of the Call

All his life our hero has been dreaming of great things, but when he finally gets the **call to adventure** he backs off. 'Actually I'm quite comfortable here. Maybe I'll go some other time.' Or similar. Think of Luke in *Star Wars* or Neo in *The Matrix*. None of us

likes leaving our comfort zone and the hero is no different. This is often when the mentor arrives in order to encourage the hero with advice and a talisman. In my *Time Travel Diaries*, Alex says to himself, 'How could I possibly go back to Roman London? I was just a kid in Year Eight with a pathetic smattering of Latin words . . .' Instead of a mentor, something else causes him to change his mind: a renewed desire for 'the desire'! Of course, some brave heroes leap to the call without hesitation. Two examples are Katniss from *The Hunger Games* and WALL-E when he grabs onto the spaceship to follow EVE.

Research

For me, one of the joys of being a writer is that I can research things I'm interested in to better describe my world and the people in it. I want to know what it was really like to live in first-century Rome or Virginia City, Nevada, in the year 1863. I'm thrilled when a book, movie or TV show convinces me that the world they're showing is accurate. So I read books, go to museums, scour the Internet and sometimes even interview an expert. I have delved deeply into a whole range of subjects from ancient Greek philosophy to the Cult of Mithras to Roman chariot races and even types of tobacco during the American Civil War. I have taken classes, travelled, attended plays, lectures and re-enactment events. I have filled dozens of notebooks and virtual photo albums. And then I have to leave out about ninety per cent of what I have learned, because you must never allow facts to clog up the story!

Warning! Don't spend so much time doing research that you don't have time to write. That is one of my tendencies.

Right Brain

'To see a world in a grain of sand, and a Heaven in a wild flower, hold infinity in the palm of your hand, and eternity in an hour.'
William Blake

The right hemisphere of your brain controls the left-hand side of the body. It also controls visual-spatial functions and is in tune with the five senses: sight, taste, smell, hearing and touch. It is the creative part of your brain, the daydreaming part. When people talk about 'imagination' I believe they mean the right side of the brain, because that's where images are formed. You need both sides equally when you write, but many people only use their bossy left brain and not the quietly imaginative right brain. One of the best ways of exercising your right brain is to daydream to music. Put on music and imagine where it takes you, what you see, hear, feel and smell. This works best with music that doesn't have words. Another way of developing your right brain is to learn memory techniques. For more on this, go to the section called ***Writing on the Right Side of the Brain*** on page 34.

Rubber Ducky

This is a fun shorthand expression for the childhood experience that made a supervillain turn evil: 'Why does he want to destroy the world? Well, it all started when he was a little boy and somebody stole his ***rubber ducky***!' Gru's rubber ducky was his mother mocking his desire to go to the moon. In one version of the DC *Superman* comics, young Lex Luthor blamed Superboy for causing his baldness, even though Superboy was saving his life. Lex was humiliated and vowed revenge. That incident was his rubber ducky. You can also use this term to describe the incident in the hero's past that haunts him. This incident in the past is often the cause of the hero's Achilles' heel. For example, Harry Potter's wounding by Voldemort. In *The Greatest Showman*, young Phineas is scorned by the father of the girl he loves because he is 'only a tailor's son'. This sparks his desire to be accepted by the posh upper classes. This flaw causes him to leave his family and friends and put himself in moral danger until he comes to his senses. The people who came up with the term 'rubber ducky' were mocking this trope, but it's funny and memorable . . . and a powerful storytelling tool.

Running Start

Script guru John Truby advises writers to give their story a running start. In other words, from the very first page the hero is on the run or in some kind of trouble. This is good because it draws the reader or watcher into the story, but it can cause problems. Until we know who our hero is, we don't really care about them. Some film-makers have a running start but make it part of the **set-up** or back story. In *Vertigo* (which some film critics think is the greatest movie ever made), our hero is shown running across the rooftops of San Francisco. But this is not the main story; it shows how he got his fear of heights (also known as 'vertigo'). In *Star Wars* a massive Imperial Star Destroyer is pursuing a small rebel ship. Inside the rebel ship an android sees a princess give a small robot something. This, again, is the **set-up** for a later **payoff**. After this you can slow down and show your hero's desire and needs. Another way to start your book with a running start is to plunge right into the middle, or ***in medias res***, as the Romans used to say. You can show an exciting scene from near the end at the beginning, then leave readers hanging from a cliff as you go back to 'It all started when . . .' in chapter two. On a side note, running starts and chases are excellent for book covers as they show the story contains tense and exciting scenes.

Save the Cat!

This is a scene that often occurs near the beginning of a story where the main character does something nice to make us like them, like save a cat stuck up a tree. When I first read about this in script guru Blake Snyder's book on screenwriting (called *Save the Cat!*) I raised a sceptical eyebrow and thought, *Really*? But that very night my husband and I randomly watched a western called *Hang 'Em High* and the first thing the cowboy does is save a calf! Not a word has been spoken but we know he's a nice guy. We know he's our hero. At the beginning of *Moana* she saves a crab. At the beginning of *The Wizard of Oz*, Dorothy risks her life to save her dog Toto. At the beginning of *Raiders of the Lost Ark*, Indiana Jones (twice) saves a guide even though he knows he was probably going to betray him. *WALL-E* saves his friend the cockroach. Hiccup doesn't kill the dragon he wounded; he saves it. And so on . . . You can do a fun twist which I call '**Kill the Dog**' to show the hero is maybe not so nice.

SET-UPS AND PAYOFFS

One of the beautiful things about rewriting is that if you have a character suddenly able to walk a tightrope or defuse a bomb you can go back and set it up in an earlier scene, explaining why they have this skill. In *How to Train Your Dragon* we see at the beginning that Hiccup is good at designing things. Later in the movie when he designs a prosthetic fin for Toothless the dragon, we believe it. In *Moana* we see early on that she has a special relationship with the ocean (which plays the role of her **faithful sidekick**), so we believe it when the ocean protects her when she is older.

Show Don't Tell

'A picture is worth a thousand words.'
Anonymous

Instead of telling your reader or viewer what is happening, show them through images. This will appeal to the right brain and make a deeper impact. One of my all-time favourite movies is *The Black Stallion*. For almost the entire second act there are no words as a shipwrecked boy attempts to make friends with a wild stallion. It is stunning and unforgettable. The opening of *WALL-E* is another genius example of a movie without dialogue for the first ten minutes. My mentor John Truby says the most important moment of a movie, the self-revelation (which I call the 'knowledge'), often occurs in silence. When writing, show how the character is feeling rather than telling us. Use **ninja description** wherever you can.

Warning! Don't go too far with showing and not telling . . . You have to tell the readers or viewers *something* or they will be completely lost, hence the need for **Basil Exposition**, **snaxposition**, etc.

SMARTPHONE SABBATH

'Being a good writer is 3% hard work and 97% not getting distracted by your devices.'
Caroline Lawrence

I love my smartphone, which is hugely useful in my writing process. I make notes on it, send myself emails with ideas so I don't forget them, listen to podcasts about movies and writing, enjoy audiobooks and keep my readers informed via social media. But the smartphone can also be a tyrant, demanding your attention. And it can be a corrupting influence, making you lazy about research. That's why I try to have a 'Sabbath rest' from my smartphone and other technology at least once a week. I'm not always successful. I just about manage leaving my phone and computer off between midnight Saturday and noon on Sunday. Twelve whole hours! But even having just that Sunday morning without technology is very liberating. It encourages me to leaf through magazine articles, my writer's notebooks and the books on my shelf.

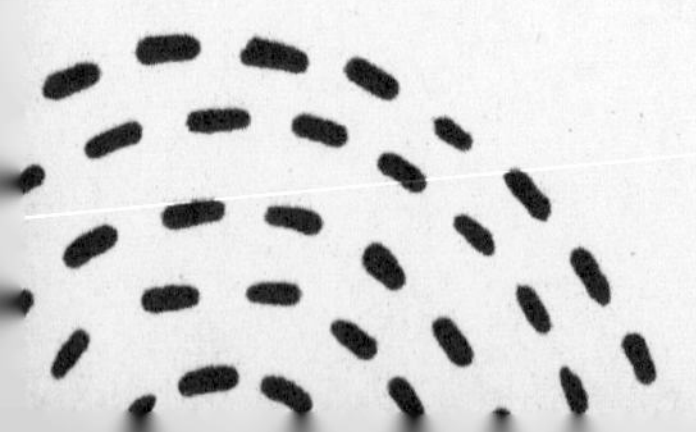

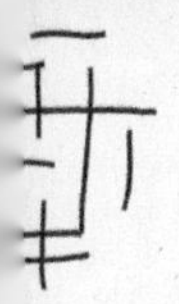

SNAxPOSiTiON

> *'A good book makes you want to go to the refrigerator.'*
>
> Caroline Lawrence

I love books which describe good meals, tasty snacks and even disgusting food. One way to keep the reader's interest engaged

in a mentor's briefing or a passage of boring exposition is to set the scene in a restaurant or cafe serving delicious food. Snacks + Exposition = Snaxposition! In *The Time Travel Diaries*, the plus-sized mentor Solomon Daisy often briefs the hero Alex as they eat and drink interesting food. A lot of snaxposition happens in the pub at Hogsmeade in Harry Potter, where plans are often discussed over Butterbeer. The heist movie *Ocean's Eight* has several scenes of snaxposition between the hero and her sidekick.

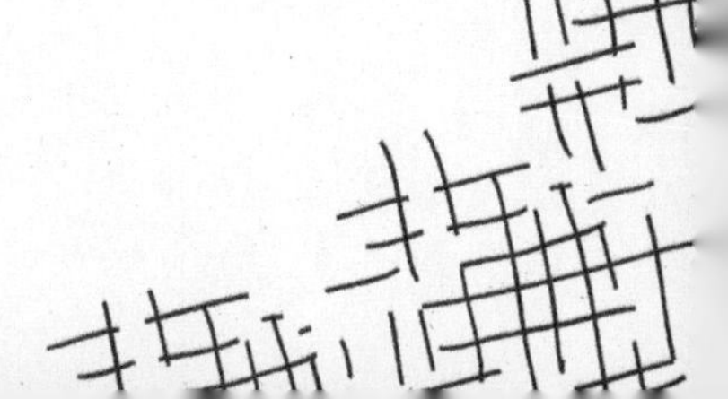

Stakes

Stakes means what is at stake if the hero does not get his desire. In *James Bond* movies the stakes are usually extremely high because the **opponent** is often an evil mastermind who wants to destroy the world. In *Avengers: Infinity War* the stakes are half the people in the entire universe. If your stakes are high, this obviously adds tension, but you can have tension even with lower stakes, if the hero really cares about them. In *The Magician's Nephew* by C. S. Lewis the hero is a boy who wants to bring a magic apple home to save his mother from dying. She's only one person – not half the universe – but we are still desperate for Digory to succeed. There is often a stage in the second act where the stakes are raised, often by the death of someone, to show how urgent the mission is. Pixar via Khan Academy say that the **primal** definition of 'stakes' is: why do we care? It doesn't need to be life and death, but you need to show it's massively important to the character. They also talk about external, internal and philosophical stakes.

Stagnation

The word 'stagnation' means a state of not flowing or moving. Think of a pond with scum on top as compared to a sparkling brook. Some of the best stories show the hero in a state of stagnation when we first meet them in their **ordinary world**. They are happy enough but are going nowhere. We feel that at best they will stagnate (like that scummy pond) and at worst they will die. At the beginning of *WALL-E* a little garbage-bot is methodically doing the same thing he's been doing for hundreds of years: cleaning up Earth's rubbish. He is like Sisyphus from Greek mythology, who was constantly pushing a boulder up a hill, only to have it roll down again. Or think of Carl Fredericksen from Pixar's *Up*, lonely in his little house, refusing to move and grieving his dead wife. At the beginning of *Star Wars*, Luke is a farm boy who dreams of fighting in the rebellion but needs to ask permission just to go into town to meet his friends. Our hero needs a wake-up call to send them on a journey which will result in the sequence of events that will help them fulfil their potential.

STORYBOARD

Storytelling is not just about words. Perhaps the most famous motto for screenwriters is **'Show Don't Tell'**! That means you show what is happening so that your readers' or audience's imaginative right brain gets to be involved. When I write, I try to 'see' each scene I'm writing, as if I were at the cinema or, better yet, an invisible witness right there so that I can smell and feel things too. A storyboard is like a page in a graphic novel or comic where you draw important scenes and what angle you see them from. If you're using your imagination, you might as well fly up in the air and look down from a bird's eye view. Or you could take a 'worm's eye view' from down low. You can get right up close or go very far away. It doesn't matter if you 'can't draw'; you are the only one who needs to see it. And it might help inspire fresh ways of telling your story. (See also ***Draw Your Characters***.)

Subject

You might already know what you want to write about. For example, your grandfather's life as a soldier. Maybe a kid like you who gets superpowers or magic abilities. Perhaps a story of love and friendship. But what if you have no idea what to write about? If your teacher or editor doesn't give you a topic, you could try brainstorming ideas on a sheet of paper. Another good way of coming up with a subject for your story is to **magpie** one of your favourite **first lines**. You'll find that as you plug in a few different words and maybe a different name you are getting an idea. It's much easier to write with a subject or title in mind, even if it's been assigned to you. See my *Sample Workshop #3* on page 47 for more details.

STRUCTURE

'Every story needs a structure, just as every body needs a skeleton. It is how you flesh out and clothe your structure that makes each story unique.'
Caroline Lawrence

To some writers and critics, structure is a dirty word. They think anything with a formula is formulaic. A few authors get down as many words as they can and then start editing bits out, a bit like the famous sculptor Michelangelo, who apparently said that every block of stone had a statue inside it and it was the task of the sculptor to discover it. That is a pretty haphazard way of writing. Many of the writers I most admire carefully plot their stories. The metaphor I have found helpful is to imagine a sculptor who starts with a wire frame, then puts clay on that, building up the shape. Sometimes they will take away some clay, but it's mainly a matter of building onto a structure. When I go into a school, I ask the kids to look around and imagine everyone in the classroom as a skeleton. 'You would all look the same,' I say, 'because you all have the same structure. It's your muscle, skin, hair and clothes that make you individuals.'

TAKE A CLASS

If you're not in school and want to write something, consider taking a class. It could be anything from bushcraft to pottery to modern dance. You will enter a fun new **world of adventure**. You will find a **mentor** in your teacher and some **sidekicks** in your classmates. In the past ten years I have taken classes in basketmaking, natural dyes, graphic novel design as well as ancient Greek and Latin. Reading Virgil's *Aeneid* in a Latin class inspired two books: *The Night Raid* and *Queen of the Silver Arrow*. It helps if you live in a city like London where there's always a lot going on, but you can do courses via the Internet too. If you're still a kid, don't despair. You can go places adults can't. You can tell us what it's like to be a cub scout or on the swim team or to attend a youth group. Maybe you think your world is 'boring'. But remember: Luke Skywalker thought Tatooine was boring too. Your **ordinary world** is as fascinating to anyone else as Tatooine is to anybody who isn't Luke Skywalker.

yes

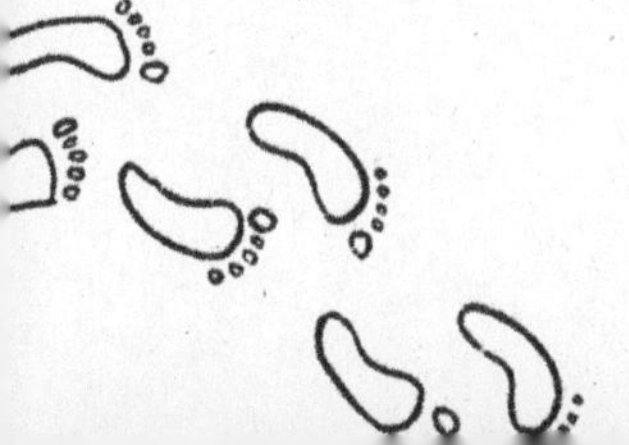

THE TALISMAN

The word 'talisman' comes from the Arabic word 'tilsam' which means a 'charm'. In storytelling, the talisman is an object – often magical – that gives the hero help just when it's most needed. The talisman also reminds the hero that they are the chosen one for the particular task. In *The Hunger Games*, the mockingjay pin is Katniss's talisman. The **mentor** often gives the hero the talisman, e.g. Obi Wan gives Luke the lightsaber, Good Witch Glinda gives Dorothy the ruby slippers and Aunt Lucy gives Paddington his Uncle Pastuzo's hat. In *The Black Stallion*, the father is a kind of mentor when he gives Alec a little Greek figurine of Bucephalus, the stallion tamed by young Alexander the Great.

TALK ABOUT IT

Some writers believe that when you have an idea and are working on a project, it's best to keep it a secret because if you talk about it you might somehow lose the urge to write about it. But I find that it's useful to tell people what you're working on. When we are immersed in the world of our story, we forget that other people don't know a thing about it. As you explain aspects of your story you have to take a mental step back to make it clear to your listener. That reminds you to make it clear to your readers too. I usually wait until someone asks me about what I'm writing and then shows interest. But Blake Snyder used to share his movie ideas with random people standing in line at Starbucks! That's even braver than the **elevator pitch**.

Theme

The theme of a story is an important idea or message that runs through it. This often reflects the author's view of life. It's always good to have an idea of what your book is about on a deeper level. Some writers believe the theme doesn't reveal itself until the story is finished. The Hollywood scriptwriting teacher Blake Snyder suggests that you 'state your theme' in the early scenes of a movie, often as something a character says to your hero. You can always go back and do this once you know what your theme is. But don't make it **on the nose** (totally obvious) like: 'You know what you need to learn? That riches don't bring happiness.' Try to hide it a little. The theme of *The Time Travel Diaries* is: 'We don't know how good we have it.' Some authors write the theme of their **WIP** as one or two words on a Post-it note and stick it above their computer so they'll keep it in mind.

THREE-ACT STRUCTURE

In his book called *Poetics*, the ancient Greek philosopher Aristotle said that every story has a beginning, a middle and an end. He was thinking of the very first Athenian dramas, which had three parts. Many Hollywood screenwriters have embraced this idea of a three-act structure. You don't have to use it, but it can help you find the shape of your story. The first act usually takes place in the hero's **ordinary world** and shows **stagnation**. Then, about a quarter of the way through the story, your hero **crosses the threshold** into the **world of adventure**. The second act is often twice as long as the first act and has a midpoint which is also the midpoint of the book. The final quarter or so is the third act. The hero often makes a **visit to death** at this point and then returns home, hopefully having learned a valuable **life lesson**. One screenwriter joked that in the first act he puts his character up a tree, in the second act he sets the tree on fire and in the third act he gets his character down again.

Threshold Guardians

Sometimes when your hero tries to leave their **ordinary world** for the **world of adventure**, they meet threshold guardians. These characters want to make it hard for your hero to cross over. Remember the stormtroopers who stop Luke and Obi-Wan in their landspeeder? Or Cerberus the three-headed hellhound from Greek mythology? They are threshold guardians. One of my favourite threshold guardians is the old bridge-keeper from the movie *Monty Python and the Holy Grail*. Although I've been writing for over twenty years I'm still trying to hone my skill. I went to hear Hollywood script guru Christopher Vogler a few years ago and he began by telling us what a pain it had been getting through customs and passport control at Heathrow airport. Then he had a revelation: he was a hero on a journey and the guys at the airport were just threshold guardians. It was the universe making sure he really wanted to come to London to teach us about story structure.

The Title

One of the hardest things about writing a book is the title. For some writers it comes easily. Others, like me, need a little help from our friends . . . and editors. One-word titles are good because a single word has impact. The title is often the hero of the story: *Shrek*, *Rango*, *WALL-E*, *Paddington*, *Moana*, *Wonder Woman* and *Black Panther* for example. Sometimes the title is the **world of adventure**, like *The Secret Garden*, *Night at the Museum* and *Jurassic World*. However, you can often get your title from one of the seven plot beats. For example:

1. Problem = *Frozen*
2. Desire = *Finding Nemo*
3. Opponent = *Jaws*
4. PLAN = *How to Train Your Dragon*
5. Battle = *Avengers: Infinity War*
6. Knowledge = *Coco*
7. New Level = *Sing*

YAY!

For my Roman Mysteries, I wanted a Classical word in the title and my editor wanted an exciting word. In the end we compromised and had one Classical word and one exciting word. For example, *The Pirates of Pompeii*, *The Assassins of Rome*, *The Enemies of Jupiter*, etc. If you can't think of a proper title, come up with a **working title**!

Torture your hero

You don't have to literally torture your hero, but don't make things easy. Give them obstacles and opponents, tests and trials. One of the reasons we read is to experience things in a virtual world rather than in real life. The first plays of ancient Greece were part of a religious festival, and according to Aristotle's *Poetics* they were thought to be cathartic, which is when you go through the agony of someone else's story in order to come out of it clean and empty and even refreshed. I have a friend who watches horror films when he's depressed and it always makes him feel better. Reading about someone worse off than yourself inspires gratitude and puts our own troubles in perspective. The best stories are **empathy machines** that arouse your impulse to be kinder to others. The problem with writing about people in pain is that we authors care about our heroes, so it's hard to hurt them. (See also **Conflict**.)

The Travelling Angel

Some heroes have no Achilles' heel. They are pretty much perfect. Screenwriters call them 'travelling angels'. They come into the community, help people with a problem and then go away. Mary Poppins is a classic travelling angel. She drops in, fixes things and then leaves. TV's The Doctor from *Doctor Who* has been a travelling angel for over fifty years and she's still going strong. Nancy Drew and many other detectives are travelling angels too. In the 2014 movie *Paddington*, the little bear from darkest Peru has no weaknesses, apart from his 'worrying marmalade habit'. He is a travelling angel who fixes the Brown family. Happily, instead of leaving at the end, Paddington Bear stays.

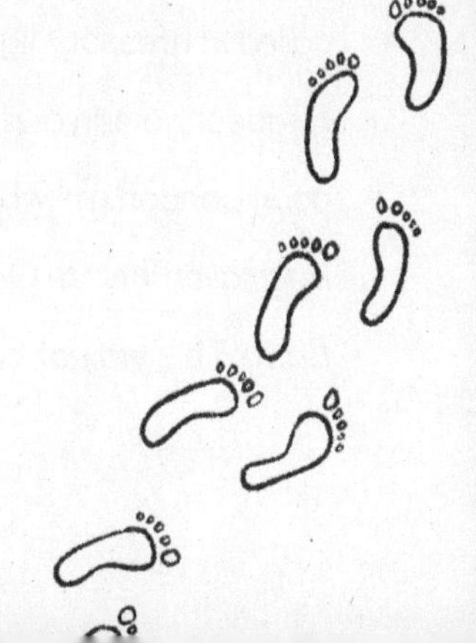

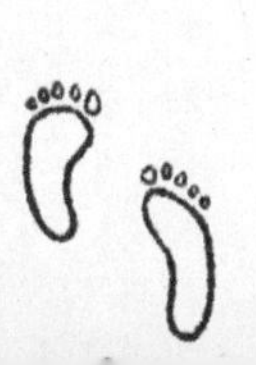

Use a Myth

My favourite myths are the Greek myths, among the most ancient stories in the world. Their authors are long dead and won't mind if you borrow those stories and make them new. George Bernard Shaw wrote a play called *Pygmalion*, in which he reimagined a king from Greek mythology as an Englishman called Professor Higgins. King Pygmalion carves a statue of his ideal woman and Henry Higgins does a makeover on a poor London girl who sells flowers. Later they made the play *Pygmalion* into an Oscar-winning movie musical called *My Fair Lady*. This way of coming up with an idea can work especially

well with ancient myths from different cultures. As Rick Riordan does in in his Percy Jackson books, you can set the myth in a modern setting. Or you can embed the myth deep in the story. I consciously worked a Greek myth into my seventeen Roman Mysteries. Each of those books included elements, themes, names and even plot points from the myth. For example, *The Twelve Tasks of Flavia Gemina* uses the Hercules myth. You can also use fairy tales, fables and folk tales. You can even use Shakespeare: the Oscar-winning musical *West Side Story* is *Romeo and Juliet* set in modern times.

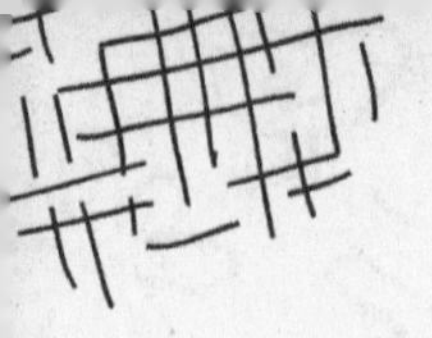

The Visit to Death

In many stories there is a moment when the hero is at his lowest, often at the **midpoint**. This goes back to Greek mythology where almost every hero visits Hades, the Greek underworld. It is here, at their bleakest moment, that the hero realises how precious life is and resolves to muster all their strength and go on. In *The Aeneid*, our hero's visit to death comes when he goes to the underworld to consult the spirit of his dead father. That occurs halfway through, in book six of twelve.

But as with **crossing the threshold**, there can be smaller examples. When Aeneas flees burning Troy and goes back to find his wife, only to see her ghost, that is a kind of visit to death. When Paddington goes down the escalator of the London Underground for the first time, that is a comical visit to death.

THE VOMIT DRAFT

I've heard a few screenwriters use this expression when talking about the first draft of their scripts. The idea is that once you've got it all down on paper then you can start to clean it up by revising and polishing it. According to Hollywood script guru Christopher Vogler, the award-winning filmmaker Francis Ford Coppola said, 'I always aim to write a bad first draft.'

When I'm writing a first draft or synopsis, I sometimes do scenes as a vomit draft. Giving myself permission to write a bad first draft I get down as much down as possible. When the voice in my left brain whines, 'That's rubbish,' I just reply, 'Of course it's rubbish; it's my vomit draft.' Writing a vomit draft is easy if you've been doing stream of consciousness **Morning Pages**.

Walking Solves Problems

I never get writer's block in the sense that I can't think what to write, but sometimes my plots get really complicated or I need to figure out how to best write a scene. In those cases I plug the problem into my head, mutter a prayer to the Great Storyteller, put on music and then walk. Something about the forward motion and the alternating of left and right feet and arms – which incidentally forces both sides of your brain to work together – never fails me. By the time I get back home, the solution has often dropped into my head. Or at least I have some alternative ideas. Or at least the feeling of being tangled in a story-ball of yarn has gone away. A couple of times it has been so bad that I actually felt trapped, like a hamster in a cage. I usually reserve mornings for writing and afternoons for walking, but on those mornings I walked. Sometimes I talk to myself as I walk in order to come up with a solution. Many other writers have told me they do the same thing. A few find release in driving or – strangely – taking a shower. However, one of the beauties of walking is that it is a good physical break from your sedentary life as a writer. It keeps you fit, fills your lungs with oxygen and gets you out into the world.

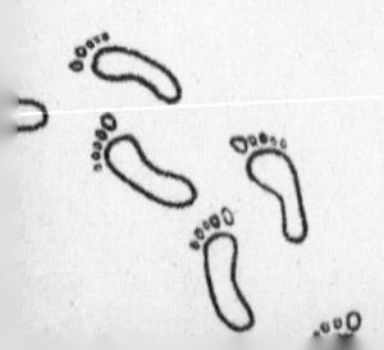

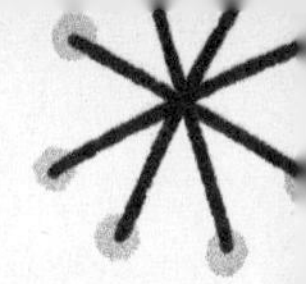

What If . . . ?

If you want to write, but don't know what you want to write about, try playing the 'What if . . . ?' game. That's where you let your imagination wander. What if a kid like me had magic powers? What if a dog could talk? What if my teacher was really a spy? What if Godzilla met Bambi? What if a clever truth-seeking girl like Nancy Drew lived in ancient Pompeii?

***Ding!* Light bulb moment!**

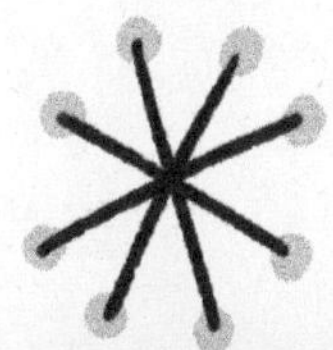

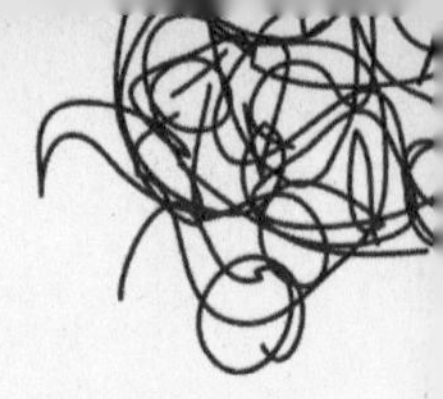

Why Write?

If you don't have to write for school and you're not writing to get rich (Ha!) then why write? Some people say they 'have to write or they would die'. Many authors say they can't imagine doing anything else. Writers from thousands of years ago to the present time want to write because it is a way of living on after you die. I write to figure out the best way to live in the world. That's why my current **WIP** is about one of the wisest men in the world, the Greek philosopher Socrates. Why was he so influential? What made him different? What if I could go back in time and meet him? Would I even like him?

Another reason to write is self-discovery. If you write enough books, you discover you keep coming back to certain themes, ideas, characters, situations and even lines of dialogue. It can help you identify and work through your problems. Writing is a kind of therapy, maybe even better than an analyst. Writing will help you to 'Know thyself!'

WIP

WIP (or W.I.P.) stands for Work In Progress. You can have several of these. I often think of my writing projects as the courses of a dinner party at different stages of preparation. The starter is ready and just needs the finishing touches. (That's the book when it's almost ready to go to print.) The main course is bubbling away on the stove. (That's my current WIP.) The dessert is waiting to be prepared. All the ingredients are ready but haven't yet been assembled. (That's my next project.) Hey! Maybe you already have some ideas about the menu for a great 'dinner party'.

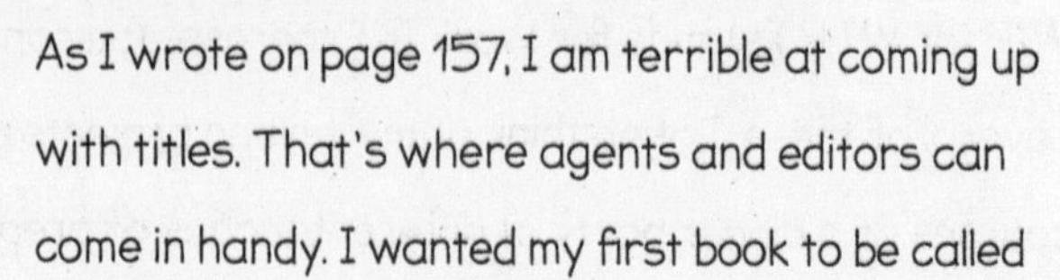

As I wrote on page 157, I am terrible at coming up with titles. That's where agents and editors can come in handy. I wanted my first book to be called *Flavia Gemina and the Three Heads of Cerberus*, but my then editor told me nobody would be able to spell 'Cerberus', and sure enough, when the art department came up with a sample cover, they had misspelled Cerberus. I wanted a Classics-related word and my editor wanted an exciting word. Finally we agreed to compromise. As a result, almost all my Roman Mysteries have one Classical word and one exciting word: e.g. *The Pirates of Pompeii*.

Some famous movies had surprising working titles: *Titanic* was going to be called *Ice Planet*; the working title of *Frozen* was *The Snow Queen*; and nobody was fooled when they were filming *The Dark Knight* as *Rory's First Kiss*, mainly to stop fans from mobbing the set and finding spoilers. Remember: the **title** often comes from one of Truby's seven beats. If you can't think of a good title, think of a bad one. After all, it's just your working title. (A 'working title' is another way of saying a temporary title.)

The World of ADVENTURE

I've written a bit about the world of adventure at the beginning of this book. It doesn't occur in all stories, but it is a great element to include if you can. Your hero **crosses a threshold** from their own **ordinary world** into a new world of adventure. This is often an upside-down world where your hero is a **fish out of water**. Once your hero is in this new world, they make friends and learn new skills and lessons. They battle the **opponent** and hopefully get some **knowledge**. Sometimes the hero stays in the new world, but often they return home with knowledge, with or without their new friends. Some of my favourite heroes who remain in the new world are Aeneas, Paddington, Theseus and Luke Skywalker. Heroes who return home are Dorothy Gale, Frodo, Moana, Nemo, WALL-E, Mr Carl Fredericksen, Marty McFly from *Back to the Future*, Miguel from Pixar's *Coco* and many more.

Write a Poem

Sometimes when I'm feeling stale or stuck, I write a poem. It doesn't have to be a long poem. It could even be a haiku, a type of Japanese poem that has strict but simple rules. A haiku must have three lines of five, seven and five syllables, making seventeen syllables in all. This makes you think about what each word is doing. It helps you get rid of padding. It reminds you to be creative with metaphor, alliteration and other poetic techniques that can make your writing pop. Here's a haiku I wrote called 'Story Cakes'.

Stories are soul cakes;
We devour them with our eyes
And they feed our lives.

And here's one called 'It Takes Two'.

Right foot's the Hero
But my humble left foot is
her Faithful Sidekick.

Write What You Know?

A very common piece of advice given to new writers is 'write what you know'. Of course this is a good idea. As I said on page 122, your world may be boring to you, but to us it's fascinating! However, if you have an amazing idea that's outside your own experience then go for it! If the characters are fantastical you can still describe their motivations and emotions according to your own experience. And if the setting is strange or foreign, you can do research. I have never lived in Ancient Athens or Roman Britain but I did lots of research to find out more about those places. More than 'write what you know', I would say 'write what you are passionate about'.

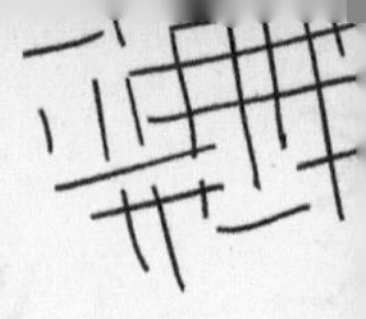

THE WRITERS' DATE

The writers' date is like **the artist's date**, but instead of going somewhere on your own, you meet with a fellow writer or wannabe writer. I regularly meet with one friend who doesn't plot out her books first but loves to talk about the process of writing. Recently we inspired each other over tea in the cafe of a furniture store. Afterwards we wandered around the shop trying to decide which of our characters would like this cushion or sit in that chair. I also get inspired by meeting with wannabe writers – both young and old – to share my tips. The universe rewards generosity; it was the day after meeting with a young writer that I got the idea for this book.

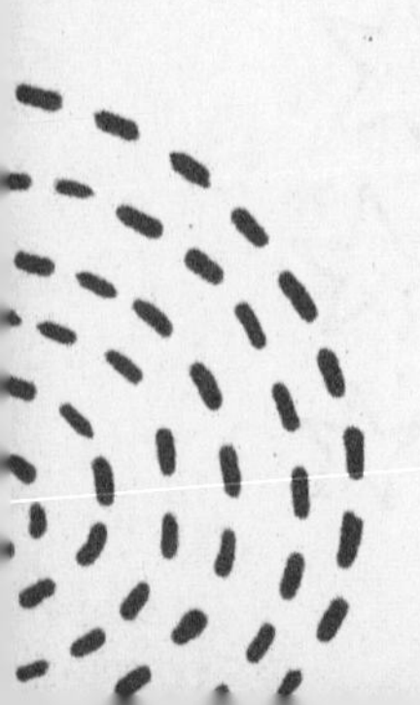

Writer's Notebook

Sometimes an idea pops into your head when you least expect it. It's good to jot it down as soon as possible. In these days of smartphones you can always dictate ideas into a notes app or email them to yourself for later, but I think every writer should have a physical writer's notebook. I carry pocket-sized ones and write with my felt-tip pen. But you could have a beautiful leather-bound one on hand-made paper and write with a fountain pen. Ideas you get in the middle of the night are sometimes gibberish but not always. I once had a **cascade of ideas** at four a.m. Luckily my writer's notebook was by my bedside table and although it was dark I scribbled them down.

WRITERS' ROOM

We're living in a Golden Age of Television and most successful shows are collaborations. A head writer or 'show runner' has a room full of writers. Together they 'beat out' the arc for the season and then work together to write the episodes, each of which will have its own arc. Often each writer will get an episode and the others will feedback and help polish it. This is an unusual way of writing because most writers are solitary people. It doesn't mean we don't have friends. It just means we are happy spending time on our own. If you are working on your own a lot, you can feel a bit isolated, so sometimes it's fun to write with others. There are writing groups all over the country that can help you with your stories. Or you can just meet up with a fellow writer for a **writers' date**.

STORIES MENTIONED IN THIS GUIDE

[book] (film) {TV}

The Aeneid [c. 19 BC]
Alice in Wonderland [1865]
All Is Lost (2013)
Austin Powers movies (1997-2002)
Avengers: Infinity War (2018)
Back to the Future (1985)
Black Panther (2018)
The Black Stallion (1979)
The Borrowers [1952]
Charlotte's Web [1952]
A Christmas Carol [1843]
Coco (2017)
Despicable Me (2010)
Doctor Who {1974 to present}
Finding Nemo (2003)
Friends {1994-2004}
Frozen (2013)
Gladiator (2000)
Goosebumps [1992-1997]
The Greatest Showman (2017)
Harry Potter books [1997 - 2007]
Harry Potter movies (2001-2011)
Honey, I Shrunk the Kids (1989)
House of Cards {2013}
How to Train Your Dragon (2010)
The Hunger Games (2012)
The Iliad [c. 800 BC]
The Incredibles (2004)
James Bond movies (1962 to present)
Jane Eyre [1847]
Jaws (1975)
Jurassic Park (1993)
Jurassic World (2015)
The Lego Movie (2014)
The Magician's Nephew [1955]
Maleficent (2014)
Mary Poppins (1964)
Mary Poppins Returns (2018)
The Matrix (1999)
Megamind (2010)
Mission: Impossible movies (1996 to present)
Moana (2016)
Moby Dick [1851]
Monty Python and the Holy Grail (1975)
Le Morte D'Arthur [1485]
Nancy Drew Mysteries [1930 to present]
Night at the Museum (2006)
Ocean's Eight (2018)
The Once and Future King [1958]
Paddington (2014)
Paddington 2 (2017)
Percy Jackson books [2005 to present]
Peter Pan [1953]
The Tale of Peter Rabbit [1901]
Pride and Prejudice (2005)
Raiders of the Lost Ark (1981)
Rango (2011)

Rocky (1976)
The Roman Mysteries books [2001–2009]
The Roman Mysteries {2007–2008}
The Roman Quests books (2016–2018)
Rosencrantz and Guildenstern Are Dead (1990)
The School of Good and Evil [2013]
The Secret Garden [1911]
Sherlock [2010 to present]
The Shining [1977]
Shrek (2001)
Sing (2016)
Star Wars (1977)
Star Wars: The Force Awakens (2015)
Star Wars: The Last Jedi (2017)
Stormbreaker [2000]
Stuart Little [1945]
Superman comics [1939 to present]
A Tale of Two Cities (1859)
Through the Looking-Glass, and What Alice Found There [1871]
The Time Travel Diaries [2019]
Toy Story movies (1995–2019)
True Grit (2010)
Up (2009)
Vertigo (1958)
The Very Hungry Caterpillar [1969]
WALL-E (2008)
West Side Story (1961)
The Wizard of Oz (1939)
Wonder (2017)
Wonder Woman (2017)
Zootropolis (2016)

Further Reading

The Anatomy of Story: 22 Steps to Becoming a Master Storyteller by John Truby

The Artist's Way by Julia Cameron

The Hero with a Thousand Faces by Joseph Campbell

Drawing on the Right Side of the Brain by Betty Edwards

Sapiens by Yuval Harari

Save the Cat by Blake Snyder

The Writer's Journey: Mythic Structure for Writers by Christopher Vogler

Writing Screenplays That Sell by Michael Hauge